D1342905

Wealth in Britain

HOUSE OF COMMONS LIBRARY

LOCATION		R Economic
AUTHOR	Rowlingson	
DATE	23 MAR 2000	

TO BE
DISPOSED
BY
AUTHORITY

House of Commons Library

54056000628880

Wealth in Britain

A Lifecycle Perspective

Karen Rowlingson
Claire Whyley
Tracey Warren

POLICY STUDIES INSTITUTE

UNIVERSITY OF WESTMINSTER

PSI is a wholly owned subsidiary of the University of Westminster

© Policy Studies Institute 1999

The Joseph Rowntree Foundation has supported this project as part of its programme of research and innovative development projects, which it hopes will be of value to policy makers and practitioners. The facts presented and the views expressed in this report, however, are those of the authors and not necessarily those of the Foundation.

All rights reserved. No part of this publication may be reproduced, stored in a retrieval system or transmitted in any form or by any means, electronic or otherwise, without the prior permission of the copyright holder.

A CIP catalogue record of this book is available from the British Library.

ISBN 0 85374 753 9
PSI Report No. 864

Typeset by PCS Mapping & DTP, Newcastle upon Tyne
Printed and bound by Athenaeum Press, Ltd., Gateshead, Tyne & Wear.

Policy Studies Institute is one of Europe's leading research organisations undertaking studies of economic, industrial and social policy and the workings of political institutions. The Institute is a registered charity and is not associated with any political party, pressure group or commercial interest.

For further information contact
Policy Studies Institute, 100 Park Village East, London NW1 3SR
Tel: 0171 468 0468 Fax: 0171 468 2201 Email: pubs@psi.org.uk

Contents

5 Conclusions 118

Acknowledgements

The research presented in this book has benefited from the help of a wide range of people. Barbara Ballard from the Joseph Rowntree Foundation provided steady support from the beginning to the end and our advisory group gave us expert advice on points of both method and substance. The group comprised: Kelvin Baynton, Personal Investment Authority; Carol Burgoyne, Department of Psychology at Exeter University; Margaret Frosztega and Liz Tadd, Households Below Average Income group at the Department of Social Security; Harriet Hall, National Consumer Council; David Hitchens, Department of Economics at Queen's University Belfast; and last but not least Paul Johnson, Institute for Fiscal Studies. As always, any errors in this book are the authors' own.

Each stage of the project required the help of a number of people. Sue Johnson in the Policy Studies Institute (PSI) library provided her usual excellent standard of help with searching databases and gathering material for the literature review.

During the qualitative research, Janet Dewes from the Field Department of MORI was in charge of helping us to recruit people for the in-depth interviews. The interviews were then carried out by Mark Bevan, Louise Brown, Jackie Goode and Marie Kennedy. It is a tribute to the skill of these interviewers that we were able to gather detailed information on people's assets – a subject which many researchers and interviewers would approach with trepidation. The interviews were then transcribed by Jackie Hall and Joe MacGowan.

The Family Resources Survey (FRS) and the Households Below Average Income variables were made available by the Department of Social Security, but the DSS bears no responsibility for the analysis or interpretation of the data reported here. At

PSI, John Forth also gave his time generously to share his expertise with handling the FRS. Advice on tackling data on endowment policies was received from Chris Pullen of the Personal Investment Authority and general comments on the analysis were received from Jo Semmence at the Department of Social Security and Stephen McKay then at the Centre for Research in Social Policy, Loughborough University and now at the Policy Studies Institute. Bernard Casey, now at the European Institute at London School of Economics, contibuted to the formulation of the initial proposal and the early stages of the research. He designed the algorithms to calculate pension and housing wealth and commented on drafts. Once again, however, the use and interpretation of the data are solely the responsibility of the authors.

When the project began, all members of the research team were working at the Policy Studies Institute. They have since moved on: Karen Rowlingson is at the School of Education and Social Science, University of Derby. Claire Whyley is at the School of Geographical Sciences, University of Bristol. Tracey Warren is at the Department of Sociological Studies, University of Sheffield.

Summary

Key issues and research methods

- Research into poverty and inequality typically concentrates on income as a measure of economic well-being, but ownership of wealth is also an important measure. The distribution of wealth is highly unequal – much more so than the distribution of income.
- Inequality in wealth is partly due to age and lifecycle effects, but within each age group, assets vary considerably with level of income and a range of other personal and structural factors.
- In this book we look at three different types of wealth: financial savings; housing wealth; and pension wealth. Financial savings represent the most liquid form of wealth, pension wealth is non-marketable and housing wealth lies somewhere between these two extremes. These three different types of assets play different roles in people's lives.
- This book reports on the links between income and wealth and is based on research which involved: a literature review; secondary analysis of the 1995/6 Family Resources Survey (FRS); and in-depth interviews with 40 families at different lifecycle stages. As well as looking at how people build up assets, the research considers the reverse of this, that is, dissaving or running down assets.

The links between income, wealth and the lifecycle

- Analysis of the FRS shows that median total assets of families in Britain in 1995/6 (including financial savings, accumulated state, occupational and personal pension wealth and net housing wealth) was over £53,000. Wealth increased with age, peaking at a median of £133,000 for 60–69 year-olds and then declining for older groups.

- Pensioner couples had the highest levels of wealth of all lifecycle groups (a median of £164,000). The second wealthiest group was middle-aged couples without dependent children. Young single people (under the age of 35) and lone parents had very little wealth (medians of under £4,000 for both groups).
- Income and wealth were very closely related – those with a gross annual income of less than £5,000 had median total wealth of about £3,000. Those on incomes of over £35,000 a year had median wealth of about £110,000.
- Although income and wealth were closely related, some groups, such as pensioners, were quite likely to be 'wealth rich but income poor'. And other groups, such as young single people and young childless couples were quite likely to be 'wealth poor but income rich'. The richest families, in terms of both income and wealth, were older childless couples, while the poorest families were young single people and lone parents.
- If we include state pension wealth in our definition of total wealth, 48 per cent of total assets were derived from accumulated pension wealth in 1995/6 (and just over half of this came from the state pension). About a third of all wealth was in the form of housing wealth, and financial savings accounted for the remaining 17 per cent of all wealth.

Knowledge about different types of asset

- According to the qualitative research, people had different levels of understanding about different forms of saving and investment. Those with most knowledge were more likely to be middle class, be actively saving and work in an environment related to personal finances. Those with less knowledge generally felt that they had enough for their current circumstances.

- There was a general lack of trust in financial advisers, stemming partly from personal experience and partly from general feelings stirred by controversy surrounding the selling of endowment mortgages in the 1980s and personal pensions in the 1990s.

Attitudes towards building up and running down assets

- In terms of their attitudes to savings, some of those interviewed during the qualitative research were *dedicated savers* who tried to save at all times. Many of these people were quite young and recently married and were at a stage in their lives when their income level enabled them to save or embark on a mortgage.
- Other people were *circumstantial savers* who believed that saving was more important at some points in their lives than others. These people lived through 'spend–save' cycles, saving for short periods when they could and then spending the money on necessary items such as holidays and things for their children. They generally had less money than the dedicated savers and so found saving more difficult throughout the lifecycle.
- A very few people said that they 'lived for the day' and never considered saving to be important. The few who did say that they 'lived for the day' mostly had no money to save in any case. Consequently, their situation determined their attitude rather than vice versa.
- Turning now to running down wealth, most people in the qualitative research said that they were keen to use up their financial savings during their retirement. Those who owned homes hoped to pass them on to their children. Apart from this, it was concern about benefiting from their assets before they died which determined most people's decisions about bequests to future generations.

Incentives and disincentives to save

- The tax system may provide incentives or disincentives to save generally, or to save in particular ways. Few people in the qualitative research understood how the tax system treats different types of assets, but there was some vague awareness about the role of National Savings, TESSAs and PEPs. Most people, however, had very little money to save and they preferred to put what little they had into what they saw as more accessible bank and building society accounts.
- There was some general awareness among the in-depth interviewees of social security rules about savings but those with most ability to save were least likely to need means-tested benefits and so these rules provided little disincentive to save. There was a similar level of awareness about the asset rules around long-term care, but there was also no evidence that such awareness had much effect on behaviour. This was mainly because people thought that they were highly unlikely to go into care. Respondents were nevertheless quick to condemn the social security and long-term care rules as penalising thrift.

Financial savings and housing wealth

- According to analysis of the FRS, one third of British families in 1995/6 had no financial savings at all. This proportion rose to three-quarters of lone parents and half of young single people. At the other extreme, almost six pensioner couples in ten and half of older childless couples, had savings with a value greater than the non-zero median of £3,700.
- The qualitative research highlighted the fact that people often saved money more through accident than by design (in other words, passively rather than actively). For example, they were given shares by their employer or by their building society when it demutualised. People also preferred methods of payment into savings or investment schemes which required little positive action. For example, they liked schemes which took money directly from wages (such as Save as You Earn

schemes) or which took money directly out of a current account (for example through a standing order).

- Housing tenure, and consequently housing wealth, was closely linked to both income and the lifecycle. In the FRS, around 80 per cent of families with incomes in deciles 7 or above were owner-occupiers. Seven lone parents in ten were renting, compared with only 13 per cent of older couples with pre-school age children. Nine young single people in ten had no housing wealth. Pensioner couples had median housing wealth of about £60,000 and half of all older couples without dependent children had housing wealth of about £49,000.

Pension wealth

- Pension wealth was also closely linked to income, age and the lifecycle. Just over half of all pension wealth was in the form of state pension assets. State pension wealth was particularly important for people at either end of the age spectrum with low and high levels of pension wealth respectively. Lone parents had about £3,000 in pension wealth – but, on average, only 10 per cent of this came from private pension provision (that is, occupational or personal pension provision).
- In the qualitative research, most of those interviewed thought that they were not currently putting enough money into a private pension. This was related to both income and lifecycle factors. For example, young people could have afforded to put more money into private pensions, but they wanted to spend and enjoy their money and thought that there was plenty of time before they retired. People with children felt that they could not afford to pay more money into private pensions because of the financial demands of having a family. Those whose children had grown up had more spare cash but felt that it was too late to make a substantial contribution to their future pension.
- The compulsory or semi-compulsory nature of occupational pension schemes was valued by many who said that they would probably be saving nothing or very little if they had not been 'forced' to do so. Personal pensions were viewed scepti-

cally as there was very little faith in pension advisers. Pensions were generally seen as a man's responsibility but there were some signs of generational changes, with young single women taking a similar view of pension provision as young single men.

1
—

Income, Wealth and the Lifecycle: an Introduction to the Issues

Research into wealth and assets is relatively unusual compared with research into income. Studies of poverty and inequality typically concentrate on income as a measure of economic well-being. However, ownership of assets is also an important measure. Oliver *et al* (1993, p.75) state that: '*Analyses of income only capture the current state of inequality, while wealth embodies the potential for examining accumulated and historically structured inequality.*' Sherraden (1991) goes further than many writers when he argues (p.294) that: '*Asset accumulation and investment, rather than income and consumption, are the keys to leaving poverty.*'

This book presents findings from a research study, funded by the Joseph Rowntree Foundation, into the relationship between income, wealth and the lifecycle. The book explores which factors, other than income, affect the accumulation and running down of assets. It also looks at the ways in which people accumulate wealth and why some people do this in different ways from others. Three main types of wealth are investigated: financial savings; housing wealth; and pension wealth. Following a review of the relevant literature, the study was divided into two parts: secondary analysis of the 1995/6 Family Resources Survey (FRS); and in-depth interviews with 40 people at different stages of the lifecycle.

Before turning to the research findings, this introduction briefly discusses some of the central issues and explains how the research was carried out.

WEALTH, WELFARE AND INEQUALITY

Defining wealth

The Royal Commission on the Distribution of Income and Wealth (RCDIW), convened from 1974 to 1979, distinguished between income and wealth on the basis of concepts of flow and stock. Thus, income was an amount of money that was received over a particular time period, whereas wealth constituted an amount that was fixed at a point in time (RCDIW, 1977). In this book, we concentrate on three broad categories of assets: financial savings, housing wealth and pension wealth. Financial savings represent liquid forms of wealth such as interest-bearing savings accounts (including bank and building society savings accounts as well as TESSAs and PEPs, stocks and shares, unit trusts and bonds). Pension wealth represents non-marketable wealth which can only be drawn upon in particular circumstances and in a particular form. Housing wealth is a liquid form of wealth but not as liquid as financial savings as the extent of its liquidity depends on the housing market. These different types of wealth play different roles in people's lives. Housing wealth provides a commodity which contributes to someone's current standard of living. Pension wealth provides a current or future income stream and financial savings provide a flexible resource which may be used in diverse ways.

It is important to note that in this book we have divided pension wealth into state pension wealth and private pension wealth (by which we mean occupational and personal pensions).

As well as looking at savings and asset accumulation, we also consider the reverse of this – that is, dis-saving. People may run down their assets to increase their income or consumption. In theory, borrowing can be considered dis-saving, although indebtedness goes beyond the scope of this project (see Berthoud and Kempson, 1993).

The distribution of wealth

The distribution of wealth in Britain is very unequal and even more unequal than the distribution of income. This is demonstrated quite graphically (in both the metaphorical and technical senses of the word) in Figures 1.1 and 1.2. Figure 1.1 shows a simple income

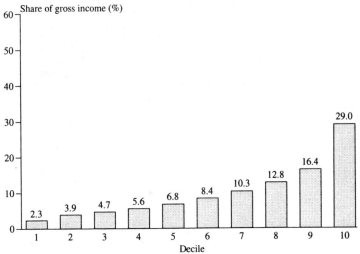

Source: 1995/6 *Family Resources Survey*

Figure 1.1   Income parade

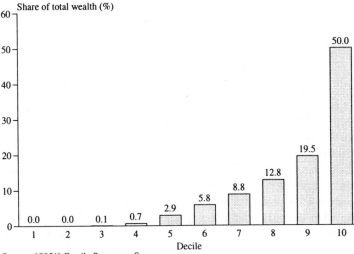

Source: 1995/6 *Family Resources Survey*

Figure 1.2   Wealth parade

parade based on the 1995/6 FRS, with the top 10 per cent of the population having more than a quarter of the income in the early 1990s. Figure 1.2 shows the equivalent wealth parade, with the top

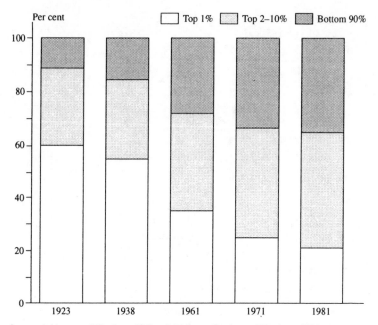

Source: Atkinson and Harrison, 1978 and Atkinson, Gordon and Harrison, 1986

Figure 1.3   Distribution of wealth

10 per cent owning half of all wealth (that is, financial, housing, occupational and personal pension wealth).

Although the distribution of wealth in Britain is still highly unequal, there was even greater inequality at the beginning of this century. Figure 1.3 shows that in 1923, the top 10 per cent owned about 90 per cent of the wealth (and the top 1 per cent owned about 60 per cent). By 1981, the share of the top 10 per cent had fallen to just over 60 per cent (Atkinson and Harrison, 1978 and Atkinson, Gordon and Harrison, 1986). However, there are doubts about whether, or to what extent, wealth inequalities have declined (Harbury, 1962; Atkinson and Harrison, 1978; Harbury and Hitchens, 1979).

This book is concerned with the distribution of wealth between different families, but the distribution *within* families is also an interesting issue, which even fewer researchers have tackled – notable exceptions being a US study by McGarry and Schoeni (1995) and a study of money in remarriage by Burgoyne and Morison (1997) in Britain.

Wealth and welfare

Wealth is an important factor to consider when investigating welfare. Sherraden (1991) argues that research on welfare which concentrates on income/consumption '*has been guided more by counting than by conceptualization*'. He argues that one of the problems with using income as a proxy for consumption/welfare is that income varies over the lifecycle. Snapshots of income levels may tell us little about the overall level of welfare of a family. And even if it were possible to measure lifetime incomes, two households with the same lifetime income may have different levels of welfare because income has been stable in one of the households and fluctuating in the other. He goes much further, to argue that assets have important effects beyond the consumption that they enable, by:

- improving household stability
- psychologically connecting people to a viable, hopeful future
- stimulating the growth of other assets such as human capital
- enabling people to focus and specialise
- providing a foundation for risk-taking
- increasing personal efficacy
- increasing social influence
- increasing political participation
- enhancing the welfare of children

To expand on some of these, ownership of assets such as housing and consumer goods also promotes the protection, care and maintenance of those assets. People with wealth also have the necessary base from which to purchase tools and skills which enable them to specialise in work and thus earn more than working in short-term, odd jobs. Risk-taking in all aspects of life – financial, social and economic – is also much more possible if people have a stock of assets. Assets can also buy greater social participation in the form of contacts, networks and information. Political participation, particularly in the US, is also constrained by lack of assets. In the early years of the republic (as in many early democracies), only landowners could vote and even now, property owners, who are more stable, are more likely to be registered to vote.

The conclusion Sherraden draws is not that income/consumption is irrelevant to welfare but that '*a consumption-only view of human welfare does not adequately reflect the complexities of human psychology, social life, or even economic behaviour'*. He argues that *'asset accumulation – stakeholding – should be encouraged by public policy'*. But far from encouraging it, policy often discourages asset-accumulation. An example of this is the application of capital means tests to entitlement of public income support benefits.

Contrary to a view which he attributes to the conservative right, Sherraden argues that it is not attitudes and values which lead to asset accumulation but that the possibility of accumulating assets leads to changing attitudes and values. The poor do not save much money because they have limited opportunities. They are not oriented towards saving because it is irrelevant to them. But if they were given greater opportunities to save, they would become more interested in asset accumulation which would, in turn, give them a stake in the future.

Economic well-being depends on both income and assets which may be drawn upon to cover the costs of various risks. It is therefore important, when considering economic security, to make a distinction between those assets which can be realised fairly easily in times of need and less marketable forms of asset which may only be realised if need is very great or very long-term.

Although much research on welfare and poverty concentrates on income, it should be remembered that some studies have considered the role of assets by devising hardship indices which take into account various factors such as ownership of cars, video recorders, washing machines and so on, as well as existence of debts (for example, Mack and Lansley, 1985, Townsend, 1979).

THE ROLE OF THE LIFECYCLE

Economic theory and the lifecycle

Lifecycle effects form the basis of economic theories of wealth distribution (Atkinson, 1971; Friedman, 1957; Modigliani and Brumberg, 1954). According to the general lifecycle theory, when people are young and on low incomes, they have had neither the time nor the ability to accumulate assets; they borrow money in the knowledge that their incomes will rise. Later on in middle age, when they are on higher incomes, they save money in the knowledge that their incomes will fall again. In the latter part of life they use up their savings. Lifecycle theory therefore predicts an 'inverted-U' or 'hump' shaped distribution of wealth across a particular person's lifetime. But this hump shape would appear in cross-section studies simply due to a combination of lifecycle effects and cohort/generation effects – as younger generations of pensioners would be better off than older ones simply because of real earnings growth rather than any lifecycle effect. Banks and Blundell (1993) argue that much of the hump shape that is evident from cross-sectional studies is attributable to cohort/generation effects rather than age or lifecycle effects.

As just mentioned, lifecycle theory predicts that, once people retire, they begin to run down their savings in an attempt to maintain their consumption patterns. The evidence suggests, however, that those retired people who do have savings do not run them down to the extent predicted by lifecycle theory. Evidence from these studies must be treated with some caution, however, as they are often based on cross-section samples rather than panels and so may be subject to cohort effects. King and Dicks-Mireaux (1982) used the Canadian Survey of Consumer Finances to demonstrate that wealth does decline after retirement, even after controlling for permanent income, but the rate of decline is less than would be predicted from a simple lifecycle theory. In Britain, there is little evidence from the Retirement Survey's panel study that people dis-save financial assets once in retirement. But the oldest respondents in the survey would have been 74 when they were followed up in 1994 and dis-saving may occur at later ages (Stears, 1998).

There are a number of reasons why retired people may not run down their assets to the extent predicted by a simple lifecycle theory. Three main reasons are:

- people's uncertainty about how long they will live
- the wish to leave money to children and/or others (a bequest motive)
- practical difficulties in converting wealth to income.

These three issues are, to some extent, intertwined. For example, difficulties converting wealth to income and uncertainty about how long you are going to live mean that bequests may not reflect a deliberate preference to leave money to others because people may not be able to access their money or may be concerned not to use up all their money long before they die. Pensions are unaffected by such uncertainties since they are paid until death, but other types of wealth are more prone to this problem. So in deciding, voluntarily, to save money in the form of a pension, people are making a decision about dis-saving – the whole point of a pension is that it is used as income after retirement and cannot be bequeathed to children or other relatives (although spouses may benefit from it after the pensioner's death).

Using up savings, whether it is financial, housing or pension wealth, is an important consideration in saving behaviour. What people anticipate spending their savings on and, perhaps more importantly, when they plan to use them up, has important implications for a range of factors, including incentives to save, the most appropriate methods of saving, the extent to which they save and the way in which they do this.

Modelling the lifecycle

Lifecycle theory is not without its limitations, but it still plays an important part in analysing the distribution of wealth. There are, however, various different lifecycle models which could be employed. Some models emphasise *stages* of the lifecycle and some emphasise *events* or *transitions*. For example, Rowntree (1901) identified five stages in the life of the labourer:

1 childhood
2 early working adulthood
3 having children
4 working life after children grow up
5 old age.

These were seen as 'five alternating periods of want and comparative plenty'.

There are various ways in which this 'Rowntree model', and other lifecycle models, may not fit people's lives perfectly:

- The chronology of events may not always occur in the prescribed order, for example, children may be born before someone starts work.
- Some stages may never be reached, for example, if people never marry or if they die early.
- There is a focus on the nuclear family and so other household members and wider networks are ignored.

The 'classic lifecycle model', which was developed in America in the 1950s and 1960s, is similar to that of the Rowntree model, with single people moving into work, then marrying, then having children, then seeing their children fly the nest, then carrying on in work until retirement age. This model, too, has been criticised because it is culturally- and time-specific, applying most to the family circumstances of white urban middle class Americans at the time when the model was developed. It is much less applicable to other times, other countries and other social classes or ethnic groups. The classic model therefore no longer applies quite so well in the late 20th century as it did earlier because of increases in:

- cohabitation and births outside marriage
- people not having children
- divorce and separation
- lone parenthood and re-marriage
- unemployment and economic inactivity among certain groups.

Some researchers have developed more sophisticated models, taking into account the age of the adults in the family and the age of the youngest or oldest child. Duration of union is also an important factor, but few models take this into account. For example, O'Higgins *et al* (1988) suggest 10 lifecycle groups and have applied their model to an analysis of 'ability to save', which shows that such models are a useful way of analysing economic differences between groups. Schaninger and Danko (1993) have conceptually and empirically compared different lifecycle models, including those developed by Duvall (1971), Wells and Gubar (1966), Murphy and Staples (1979) and Gilly and Enis (1982). They evaluated these models according to how far they:

- identified homogeneous categories
- maximised between-group variation
- classified nearly all households
- resulted in a fairly small number of sufficient size categories.

The result was that the Gilly-Enis model was the most powerful predictor of consumption patterns, leisure activity and attitudes of men and women. This model also had the advantage of including virtually everyone. It used living arrangements rather than marital status to classify couples/single people and so could incorporate cohabitation. Table 1.1 shows the 10 lifecycle groups of interest in our data, based on the Gilly-Enis model. It begins with young single adults ('young' being anyone between 16 and 35). Older single people are those between the ages of 35–64 with no dependent children. The next group is young childless (married or cohabiting) couples where the woman is under 35 and there are no dependent children. Lone parents comprise the fourth group, followed by young (married or cohabiting) couples with pre-school age children. The next group of older couples with pre-school children is similar to the last except that the woman in the couple is aged 35 or more. Then all couples with school-age children are put together for the seventh group. The next group comprises older childless couples (aged between 35–64) who have no dependent children – some of these may have had children in the past and so be in an 'empty-nest phase', others may have never had children or, at least, not with each other. Those aged 65 or over are divided into couples and singles. Although we have used the term 'pensioner' to describe these groups, they may still have paid jobs and some of those in the other groups may have retired early. The term is therefore used as a convenient shorthand for those aged 65 or more.

The major part of the quantitative analysis in this report is based on an examination of the income and wealth of lifecycle groups. Information on individuals' characteristics is used to create the lifecycle groups of the Gilly-Enis (1982) model. The age of the 'head' of the family ('person one' on the questionnaire) was used to categorise most families but the age of female partners in couples was used to classify some units, such as young couples. Note that the head of the family could equally be the female partner in our creation of lifecycle groups, but in most families the head was actually the male partner.

Table 1.1   Gilly-Enis lifecycle groups

Short title	Explanation	Percentage of families in British population	Sample size in the Family Resources Survey, 1995/6
Young singles	People aged 16–35 not married or cohabiting	17.2	5260
Older singles	People aged 35–64 not married or cohabiting	12.2	3817
Young childless couples	Couples aged 16–35 with no dependent children	4.2	1306
Lone parents	Lone parents with dependent children	6.5	2029
Young couples, young children	Couples with women aged under 35 and pre-school children (aged under 6)	7.4	2300
Older couples, young children	Couples with women aged 35 or more and pre-school children (aged under 6)	2.8	860
Couples, school-age children	Couples with school-age children – child aged six or more	10.5	3258
Older childless couples	Couples aged 35 to 64 with no dependent children	15.1	4661
Pensioner couples	Couples aged 65+	9.6	2968
Single pensioners	People aged 65+ not married or cohabiting	14.5	4568

Source: 1995/96 *Family Resources Survey*

Table 1.1 also shows the distribution of families amongst these lifecycle groups. Some groups are clearly more common in the British population than others. For example, 17 per cent of the population are young single people, 15 per cent are older childless couples and about 15 per cent are single pensioners. The smallest groups, according to this model, are older couples with pre-school children (3 per cent) and young childless couples (4 per cent). Even though these represent quite small proportions in

the population, the large FRS sample means that we have sufficient numbers in each category for reliable analysis.

ATTITUDES AND BEHAVIOUR

Although the lifecycle has an important effect on the distribution
of wealth, it cannot explain all inequalities in wealth. As we shall
see, assets vary considerably with level of income within each age
and lifecycle group, and a range of other personal and structural
factors may also be important, such as:

- attitudes to saving, spending and borrowing
- time preference and risk avoidance
- uncertainty of length of lifetime
- level of inflation and interest rates
- degree of economic insecurity
- level of state provision of welfare
- treatment of assets by tax and social security systems
- availability of saving schemes and credit.

Many of these might, in turn, be a function of age, generation,
gender, class, education or ethnicity. This section explores some
of these factors.

Cultural views and the level of saving

There are strong moral dimensions to financial behaviour which
vary between cultures and over time. In 19th Century Britain,
thrift was promoted by charitable institutions as a way of increasing the living standards of the poor and, in so doing, reducing
calls on charitable resources. A similar process exists today,
whereby the state promotes saving and self-help as a means of
reducing dependence on social security. Lea *et al* (1987) point out
that advertisers are often criticised for tempting people to spend,
but banks are rarely accused of tempting people to save. Indeed,
the very notion of 'tempting' people to save seems absurd in our
culture. But at other times or in other cultures, saving is not
universally considered particularly virtuous. Conspicuous
consumption and the giving of gifts is sometimes seen as more
important than 'hoarding'. Some elements of this remain in our

culture today, with villainous cultural icons such as 'Scrooge'. Those who save excessively are often labelled negatively as 'mean' or 'tight' with their money. So saving is generally regarded positively but generosity is also valued. A number of studies about attitudes to saving have been carried out by psychologists. See Warneryd (1998) as an introduction to this field of research.

Following on from Keynes (1936), many reasons to save have been identified, such as:

- to provide for predictable future periods of low income (such as retirement) or high consumption costs (such as children)
- as a precaution against unpredictable periods of low income (such as unemployment) or high consumption costs (in the case of illness)
- to provide positive real returns which might outweigh the costs of forgoing current consumption
- to enable the future purchase of a particular item or
- to make a bequest.

People may also save as a goal in itself (Keynes called this *'the instinct of pure miserliness'*.)

Evidence suggests that individuals in Britain and America save much less than those in many other OECD countries. For example, in 1990–91, the personal financial savings rate in Britain was 3.9 per cent and in America 6.3 per cent, compared with 10.4 per cent in Canada, 12.2 per cent in Germany and 15.7 per cent in Italy (Poterba, 1994). A number of possible reasons for these differences has been suggested, including:

- Savings in some countries such as Britain take the form of accumulating housing or pension wealth rather than financial assets, and tax systems may encourage this.
- Demographic profiles of countries may differ such that certain countries will have a greater proportion of people at an age where saving is more common.
- Countries may have different credit regimes which either encourage or discourage saving.
- Different levels and types of tax or social security systems may affect the personal savings rate.
- Lifetime income profiles may differ between countries.

Whatever the cause of the lower personal financial savings rate in Britain and the US, some (for example, Bernheim and Scholz, 1992) argue that not only is the personal savings rate relatively low in the US but that it is too low in absolute terms. As they conclude: '*Many Americans, particularly those without a college education, save too little*' (p.37). It has been argued, however (Banks *et al*, 1997), that there is no evidence, either at an aggregate level or individual level, that people in Britain save too little. For example, the personal sector savings rate has now risen (compared with the very low level experienced in the mid and late 1980s) and those who are not saving are generally on low incomes and have high consumption needs.

As far as pensions are concerned, evidence suggests that people in Britain are not putting enough money into private retirement provision (that is, occupational or personal pensions). Findings of a survey by Barclays Life showed that there was a huge gap between people's expectations of retirement and the reality. Three-quarters of working adults expected to have a standard of living which was equal to, or better than, that which they hoped to enjoy at the peak of their working lives. But current pensioners were not experiencing such high standards of living and more than two thirds said that they had not planned adequately for retirement (Barclays Life 1996). People were simply not saving enough to have the level of income which they both wanted and expected in retirement. In another study, 43 per cent of new retirees from the Retirement Survey said that they had not saved enough for retirement (Stears 1998).

There is clearly an ongoing debate about whether people in Britain accumulate enough assets. There is no doubt, however, that asset accumulation is very unequal and that many people, later in life, do not think that they have accumulated enough money to sustain the level of living standards that they wish to enjoy.

The impact of the taxation system

As argued above, there may be a number of factors which affect the distribution of wealth, and one of these is the system of taxation. The overall structure of the tax system may have some impact on savings. For example, wealth taxes may create disincentives to save and the Conservative government in 1996 committed themselves to reducing or even abolishing inheritance tax. Capital

Table 1.2   Tax treatment of assets in 1997

Asset	Tax treatment
Interest-bearing accounts	Saving out of taxed income All interest income taxed No tax on withdrawal
TESSAs and PEPs	Saving out of taxed income No tax on fund income No tax on withdrawal
Stocks and shares	Saving out of taxed income Income tax on all dividends Capital gains tax on real gains over £6,500 pa
Owner-occupied housing	Saving mainly out of taxed income (MIRAS being withdrawn) No tax on imputed income from owner-occupation No capital gains tax
Pensions	Tax relief on contributions No tax on fund income Taxed withdrawal and tax-free lump sum

Source: Banks *et al*, 1997

Gains Tax has also become less onerous since 1979 and it is now only a tax on real gains, therefore counting out inflation.

Within any income tax system, income from different types of savings may be treated more or less favourably, creating incentives or disincentives to save in particular ways. This variable treatment is known as 'fiscal privilege'. The most 'fiscally privileged' or advantageous forms of saving are those attracting tax relief; in other words, where money saved can be set against income tax, such as is the case with respect to pension contributions and mortgage repayments. Savings which are tax exempt (that is, on which the interest earned is untaxed), such as TESSAs (Tax exempt special savings accounts) are less privileged than those which attract relief. But they are more privileged than savings on which the interest is taxed (such as bank and building society accounts). Table 1.2 summarises how different types of assets are treated by the tax system.

In the 1980s, two schemes were introduced to encourage saving by providing favourable tax treatment. These were

Personal Equity Plans (PEPs), which were introduced in 1987, and TESSAs, which became available from 1991. Income from PEPs and TESSAs was not taxed, but these schemes were still less favourably treated than owner-occupied housing and private pensions (which attracted tax relief). But PEPs and TESSAs were more fiscally privileged than ordinary savings accounts, which were taxed. Take-up of PEPs was initially slow, leading to reforms in the system to make them even more attractive. In 1993/4, 1.6 million PEPs were taken out, and by 1996 PEPs accounted for about £25 billion of personal wealth (Banks, 1997). When the first TESSAs were rolled over in 1995, there were 4.5 million live accounts in the UK, with stocks of wealth amounting to £28 billion. There is also debate as to whether the introduction of the schemes has encouraged people to save more money than they would otherwise have done or whether they have just switched their savings from less favourably treated schemes to TESSAs and PEPs. Research in the US on the introduction of fiscally-privileged saving schemes, such as Individual Retirement Accounts, has produced very mixed results. Banks (1997) concludes that about a quarter of the funds invested in these accounts would not have been saved otherwise. In April 1999, the government replaced TESSAs and PEPs with Individual Savings Accounts (discussed later in this book).

The impact of the social security system

The social security system may have a number of effects on saving behaviour. Feldstein (1974) argued that social security significantly depressed private savings because there was little need to make precautionary saving if the system provided income in time of sickness or old age. But people pay National Insurance and income tax towards social security so they are, in some way, saving; and even if social security depresses precautionary savings, this may mean that money is diverted to savings for other purposes – perhaps house purchase. There is considerable disagreement about the effect of social security on saving. Cagan (1965) and Katona (1975) found that occupational pension scheme members saved slightly more than non-members but Munnell (1976) found contrary results.

Another way in which the social security system may affect saving behaviour is in the particular rules of the system. For example, the capital rules on most means-tested benefits act, in theory at least, to discourage saving since those with more than a certain amount of capital are not eligible, or only eligible for a reduced amount of benefit. Similarly, there is also a disincentive to invest in an occupational pension since this is then offset against pensioners' income support and housing benefit, leaving some people no better off than if they had not taken out an occupational pension at all. This is sometimes referred to as the occupational pension trap (Walker, Hardman and Hutton, 1988). Elderly people with property and other forms of wealth may also have to use up these assets to pay for local authority care. This issue was partly addressed in the 1995 budget, when asset limits were raised. An inquiry into the costs of long-term care carried out by the Joseph Rowntree Foundation (1996) recommended that the costs of care should be met through universal insurance rather than private insurance or general taxation, but that there should also be means-testing to cover the 'hotel' costs associated with care (that is, accommodation and other such costs).

There have been various studies which have investigated the role of means-tested benefits in creating a disincentive *to work*, but the disincentive *to save* has received less attention. The extent of the disincentive to save will depend partly on knowledge of the rules about capital limits – clearly, those who do not know about these rules will not be discouraged from saving because of them. And there will only be a disincentive on those who have the ability to save – many people do not have enough income to be able to save, regardless of whether or not there is a disincentive.

In recent years, the state has increasingly withdrawn from areas of welfare provision including earnings-related pensions and mortgage interest payments for unemployed people. Many people do not have enough income to be able to build up assets but, for those who do, assets may have become increasingly important as one form of private 'insurance' against future uncertainty of income. For example, there may be increasing demand for long-term care provided outside of the family. Only about 5 per cent of elderly people are currently receiving care in an institutional setting in the UK – above the age of 85, the figure rises to 22 per cent (Hennessy, 1995). Although these are relatively small numbers, these numbers may rise in the future and yet few people take out insurance to pay for such care. In Britain, only 1,000 people had insurance policies for long-term health care in October 1992.

RESEARCH METHODS AND CONTEXT

The aim of the research presented in this book was to analyse the distribution of income and wealth (and the links between these) across different lifecycle groups. The research also aimed to explore people's knowledge about the different ways of accumulating wealth. Finally, it aimed to investigate views and decision-making with regard to building up and running down assets. Two main research methods were used to achieve these aims, as outlined here.

Secondary analysis of the Family Resources Survey

The quantitative analysis was based on data from the *Family Resources Survey* (FRS) of 1995/96. The FRS is a major new data set sponsored by the Department of Social Security (DSS). It is very apt for this research, as the data available are far superior to those previously available on financial resources. The survey collects information from a representative sample of 26,000 households in Britain. Within these households, information is collected on 47,000 adults and 16,000 children. As a result of this very large sample size, reliable information on small sub-groups can be obtained. Moreover, the FRS includes the most extensive and reliable financial data on both income and assets. Income from employment, from benefits, from pensions and so forth are all available. Furthermore, information on both levels and different types of assets have been collected, such as financial wealth and housing wealth. Unfortunately, the FRS cannot provide information on the very small proportion of 'super-wealthy' groups as these rarely take part in surveys. Similarly, a problem with the FRS is that there is no information on the value of second homes. Second homes (and third homes, etc) will add a substantial amount to the overall wealth of some families who already have high levels of housing assets, but this will only be a small proportion of families. However, this small group is very different from the bulk of people with assets and so the absence of information on them is not a particular problem for this study.

The FRS allows information on income and assets to be analysed against a large selection of family characteristics such as age and sex of family heads and numbers and ages of any children. Although this book talks about families and their finances, the main quantitative analysis in the FRS was actually at the level of 'benefit unit', a DSS term which is quite close to commonsense ideas of 'nuclear family' (Department of Social Security, 1996: 5).

Detailed information about the quantitative analysis is provided in Appendices B and C to this report. But it is worth mentioning here that Households Below Average Income (HBAI) variables were used to calculate income. These variables were used because the FRS asks many detailed questions about income and the HBAI variables are the tried and tested measures devised and used by government statisticians to provide official evidence about the extent of inequality in Britain. The HBAI variables combine income from all the different sources asked about in the questionnaire.

Although the FRS provides some of the best current data on wealth that exist, it still has a number of important limitations and so a number of 'statistical health warnings' must be given. For example, some assets, such as financial assets, were directly available from the FRS, but only if the value was between £1,500 and £20,000. The savings of those with assets outside of this range were calculated indirectly using information about interest from savings. Pension and housing wealth also had to be calculated indirectly and such indirect calculations of data do affect the reliability of the information provided. For example, there is evidence that people cannot give an entirely accurate value of their housing wealth when asked directly (Holmans and Frosztega, 1996) and this information was used by us (along with other information, for example about council tax bands). However, the assumptions for making indirect calculations were considered carefully and full details are given in the appendices to this report.

In-depth interviews with 40 families at different lifecycle stages

The qualitative research involved in-depth interviews with 40 families at different stages of the lifecycle: young people without children; families with children; 'empty nest' or pre-retirement families without dependent children; and retired people. Qualitative research never aims to provide a representative picture of people's views and decision-making but it can indicate the range of different attitudes and behaviours.

The sample design ensured that only those with some ability to build up or run down assets would be included in the study. For example, among those groups of working age, only those families with at least one wage-earner were considered for interview. There were also quotas to ensure a reasonable number of owner-occupiers. A mix of families with different income levels and social class backgrounds was also ensured through the use of quotas. Interviewing took place in August 1997 and ran smoothly despite concerns that the nature of the study might deter people from taking part or from being open about their assets. Respondents were recruited door-to-door and in the street by fully briefed recruiters from MORI. They were then interviewed by experienced interviewers who had been personally briefed by the research team. It is a tribute to the quality of our interviewers that we have such detailed information about people's assets but it should also be noted that such information is not as difficult to collect as is often supposed.

The most obvious type of analysis to conduct with the in-depth interviews would be to compare the four lifecycle groups to see whether the groups conform to lifecycle theory. However, the sample was not selected to be typical of lifecycle groups in general, only of those with some assets or some potential to build up assets. Furthermore, as we interviewed a cross-section sample of lifecycle groups, generational effects will also be important; we cannot assume that one group will become like an older group in the future. An added complication is the variable social class mix of the lifecycle groups: the older couples without dependent children were slightly more working class than the other groups and this must be taken into account when making comparisons.

Having outlined all the warnings, it is nevertheless instructive to compare different lifecycle groups in terms of their attitudes and experiences of owning different types of assets. Full details of the qualitative methods are available in Appendices D and E of this report.

Context of the research

Before looking at the research findings, it is important to bear in mind the context within which people were interviewed in-depth about their attitudes and behaviour. The qualitative fieldwork was carried out in August 1997, at a time when the economy was generally good with falling unemployment and low inflation. In the July budget, the government had announced the introduction of Individual Savings Accounts from 1999, although very few details had been given about them. Similarly the government had announced a review of pension provision but had said little about its expected outcomes. The mis-selling of personal pensions had been in the news recently as the government had 'named and shamed' a large number of companies for advising people to take out personal pensions when it was not necessarily in their best interests to do so. A number of building societies had de-mutualised and thus become public limited companies, which meant that large numbers of people had enjoyed 'windfalls'. As far as housing wealth was concerned, mortgage interest rates had been rising slowly, but were still fairly low, and the housing market was enjoying a modest recovery, particularly in some regions such as London. Negative equity was much less of a problem than it had been at the start of the decade.

2

The Links Between Income, Wealth
and the Lifecycle

Although the lifecycle is a very important concept used in theoretical economic modelling of asset accumulation and reduction, there have been few recent empirical studies which have employed this concept. There has, however, been an important recent study by the Institute for Fiscal Studies (IFS) which analysed the relationship between income, wealth and age. This study found that median marketable wealth in Britain (financial assets and housing wealth net of mortgages) was £30,000 in 1991 but this figure rose to nearly £70,000 for families with gross incomes over £35,000 (Banks, Dilnot and Low 1994). The study also found that over half of all households had financial wealth of £455 or less. And median financial wealth was under £500 for those earning less than £17,500. Those earning between £17,500 and £25,000 had slightly more than £500 in financial wealth. But the big increase in wealth came among those earning more than £25,000 (about a fifth of the sample). There were striking patterns in the relationship between wealth and age – wealth increased until retirement age and then fell. This confirms general economic theory about the relationship between wealth and the lifecycle (discussed in the previous chapter). When income, wealth and age were analysed together, the study found that wealth rose by age within each income level and by income within each age band. There was therefore a large concentration of wealth among high-income older households.

In this chapter we investigate the overall links between income, wealth and the lifecycle, drawing on analysis of the

1995/6 *Family Resources Survey* (FRS). We begin by presenting a picture of the links between income and the lifecycle and then describe the main sources of income which different lifecycle groups relied on. We then turn to the links between wealth and the lifecycle and present a matrix of the links between income and wealth. The chapter ends with details of the distribution of different sources of wealth.

INCOME AND THE LIFECYCLE

In 1995/96, the median gross income for all families stood at approximately £260 per week. The main income variable used in this analysis was the derived variable: total gross income of the family before housing costs, which was provided by the DSS Households Below Average Income (HBAI) project. Income included: gross earnings from any employment; gross earnings from self-employment; gross investment income; gross occupational pension income; benefit income; private benefit income; and any miscellaneous income such as that from child maintenance, educational grants, baby-sitting, mail-order agencies and so forth.

It should be noted that there are a number of income/wealth links when measuring income. For example, we included pension income in our total income variable but we did not count pension contributions as negative income. This is because pension contributions are expenditure and we did not count any forms of expenditure in our calculations. Nevertheless it is important to be aware of the income/wealth links and of the method we used to calculate income.

Gross income was used rather than net income for three main reasons. First, the variable for total income included some elements (such as gross occupational pension income) for which it would be difficult to calculate net income. Second, later in the report we refer to annual income and it is more common to talk about gross annual income than net annual income. Finally, comparisons with the IFS study mentioned above can only be made if gross income is used. To some extent the choice of gross or net income is not crucial, as we are more interested in the distribution of income than the absolute amounts.

Table 2.1   Gross weekly income of families by age group of head of family

| | | | | | Ages | | | | |
	16–19	20–29	30–39	40–49	50–59	60–69	70–79	80+	All
Base	1208	5670	5702	4972	4079	3909	3650	1937	31127
					£s				
Median income	127	302	321	351	342	222	180	177	259
Mean income	163	340	405	422	418	294	224	211	341

Source: 1995/6 *Family Resources Survey*

Income was then equivalised to take into account different family sizes (using the 'McClements' equivalence scale – see Joseph Rowntree Foundation Inquiry into Income and Wealth, Volume 2, 1995: Chapter 1, for details of this scale).

In much of the analysis we refer to means and medians as a way of presenting average figures. The mean is the more commonly used type of average, but it is less appropriate when looking at income and wealth which have heavily skewed distributions (that is, a large proportion of the population have very little income and wealth, and a small proportion have a great deal). Other distributions such as that for height and weight are not so skewed, as most people fall in the middle with small proportions at the bottom and top. The median, unlike the mean, is not affected by a few extremely high values, such as the super-wealthy, because it takes the mid-point of the distribution. Median wealth is therefore lower than mean wealth and gives a better idea of typical values. However, averages only provide one summary figure and so we have also used deciles to give more information about the distribution of income and wealth.

We can see from Table 2.1 that, as just mentioned, income was highly skewed. Indeed the mean gross income of £341 per week was pulled up by very high weekly incomes of some families and was almost a third higher than the median. As a result of this skewedness, average income levels varied dramatically for different groups in the sample according to the age of the head of the family (head of the 'benefit unit', to be precise). For example,

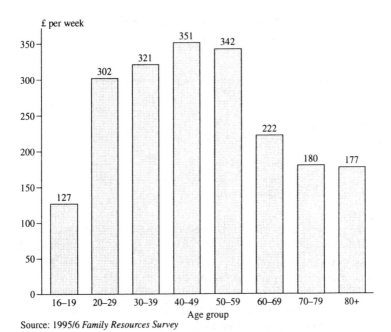

Source: 1995/6 *Family Resources Survey*

Figure 2.1   Median weekly income by age group

median gross income levels for different age groups ranged from a weekly minimum of £127 per week for 16–19-year-olds to a maximum of £351 for 40–49-year-olds. Again, as expected, the income distribution by age was in the shape of an inverted U (see Table 2.1 and Figure 2.1). This distribution shows that income levels were low for families headed by younger people, rising to a peak for families headed by 40–49-year-olds and falling off again as people approached and passed retirement age. As argued in Chapter 1, however, this inverted U or hump shaped distribution is, at least in part, due to generational/cohort effects.

These findings on age are reflected in Table 2.2, which looks at income deciles – almost half of 16–19-year-olds fall within the bottom 10 per cent of the income range.

The income levels of differing lifecycle groups also provide a picture in which median income rises until retirement age is approaching (Table 2.4). In addition, this lifecycle analysis demonstrates clearly the negative impact of young children on families' income levels – no doubt because it depresses the employment-

Table 2.2   Gross income deciles by age group of head of family

	Ages								
	16–19	20–29	30–39	40–49	50–59	60–69	70–79	80+	All
Poorest (decile I)	46	14	8	7	7	7	7	10	10
Deciles II–IX	54	78	77	77	77	87	91	88	80
Richest (decile X)	1	9	15	16	15	6	2	2	10

Source: 1995/6 *Family Resources Survey*

related income of women. The negative impact occurs even after equivalising income using the McClements scale. The presence of young, pre-school age children has long been associated with lower labour force activity of their mothers. If women with young children are in paid work, they are much more likely to be in part-time jobs than in full-time ones. Working part-time is clearly associated with lower weekly earnings, but part-timers also suffer distinct disadvantage in their hourly pay rates compared with female full-timers (Fagan and Rubery, 1996; Hakim, 1996; Martin and Roberts, 1984; Osborne, 1996; Rubery *et al*, 1994). Therefore, families who have young children are interesting groups for income analysis.

As mentioned above, the skewedness of the data leads us to use median income levels to cope with the effects of extreme outliers on average incomes. However, this skewedness is actually part of the picture that we are interested in. In other words, we are also interested in those families with the very highest and the very lowest incomes. Grouping gross income into deciles, it is possible to see quite clearly which lifecycle groups are in the very top income deciles and which are at the very bottom of the income distribution. The decile analysis serves to confirm the findings so far. In Table 2.4 (and Figure 2.2), it is apparent that the group with the highest median incomes, the young childless couples, are also the group most likely to be found with incomes in the top decile.

Table 2.3 Gross weekly income by lifecycle group

| | | | | | —— Lifecycle group —— | | | | | | |
	Young singles	Older singles	Young childless couples	Lone parents	Young couples, young children	Older couples, young children	Couples, school-age children	Older childless couples	Pensioner couples	Single pensioners	All
Median income	283	281	504	165	288	347	322	383	194	181	259
Mean income	322	377	542	206	350	428	373	463	258	219	341
Base	5,260	3,817	1,306	2,029	2,300	860	3,258	4,661	2,968	4,568	31,127

Table 2.4 Gross income deciles by lifecycle group

| | | | | | —— Lifecycle group —— | | | | | | |
	Young singles	Older singles	Young childless couples	Lone parents	Young couples, young children	Older couples, young children	Couples, school-age children	Older childless couples	Pensioner couples	Single pensioners	All
Poorest (decile I)	24	10	3	8	8	6	7	5	6	9	10
Decile II–IX	67	75	71	91	85	79	83	76	90	90	80
Richest (decile X)	9	15	26	2	7	15	10	19	2	2	10

Source for both tables: 1995/6 *Family Resources Survey*

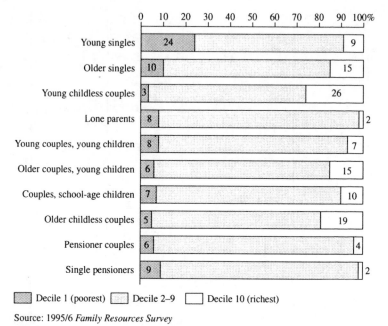

Decile 1 (poorest) · Decile 2–9 · Decile 10 (richest)

Source: 1995/6 *Family Resources Survey*

Figure 2.2   Income deciles by lifecycle groups

Income levels and lifecycle groups

By far the highest income families were the young childless couples: couples with no dependent children who were 'headed' by a person aged 16–35. Their median gross weekly income was just over £500 (Table 2.3). Although analysis at the level of family does not allow the income contributed by each individual within the family to be compared, this result does tend to suggest that high incomes for young childless couples arise from the fact that both members of these couples are in paid work. Both are probably in full-time jobs. A particular feature of these double-income-and-no-kids, or 'DINKY' families, is that the women are more likely to have had labour market careers which have been uninterrupted by child-bearing and child-rearing and therefore their employment-related income is likely to be higher than that for women who are mothers.

Characteristics of other high-income groups also reflect the importance of women's contributions to household finances and the negative impact of children on women's income potential. The ages of women's children are strongly associated with women's patterns of labour force participation in two ways: the younger the children, the lower women's participation rates, and the lower the proportions of female employees working full-time – Glover and Arber (1995) argue that the effects of the age of the youngest child on women's employment patterns differ for women from higher and lower occupational classes. Although lying at some distance behind the young childless couples' incomes, three types of family have relatively high median incomes of over £300 a week. These high earners are first, the older childless couples; second, the couples with school-age children; and third, the older couples with pre-school age children. The first group have no dependent children and the youngest dependent children of the second group are beyond school age. As a result, these two lifecycle groups will experience fewer child-related obstacles to women's entry into paid work. The groups are likely to consist of dual earner couples, albeit possibly with the female partner in a part-time job if she has returned to the labour market after bringing up a child. Notably, if women are not employed at this stage, then this is often linked to the high incomes of their partners.

The third type of families with weekly incomes over £300 are the older couples where women are aged at least 35 and have a pre-school age child. Their weekly income of £347 a week is substantially higher than that of young couples with similarly-aged children (£288). However, the outcome can be partly explained by two factors. First, as the women and men are older, this means, for men especially, that they will probably have more years of labour market experience than younger men (and therefore higher wages). Second, and importantly, the outcome may be a result of the emergence of new patterns in women's employment trajectories and in the new ways increasing groups of women are combining their home and employment lives today.

Today, some women are delaying having their first child until their thirties. Indeed, there was a 70 per cent increase in the proportions of first births to women aged over thirty between 1980 and 1990 (McRae, 1997). These women have had more years to establish themselves in the labour market, and research has shown that, on having children, these women are less likely to leave their jobs. Instead, they take paid maternity leave (Jacobs, 1997; McRae, 1994; Macran *et al,* 1996) and often return to their old jobs on a full-time basis. However, even if women in older couples with pre-school age children return to a part-time job, many actually return to their old job but negotiate the possibility of working fewer hours there. In summary, they avoid the pay penalties associated with downward mobility into the part-time labour market. Their earnings contribution to the household is more protected and this goes some way to accounting for the higher income of the families of which they form a part.

Moving onto the other end of the income distribution, the very lowest income groups are those headed by people of pension age and by lone parents. Lone parents had the lowest incomes of all and received a median weekly income of only £165 (see Table 2.3). As we shall see in the next section, the two groups of retired people and lone parents owe their low income to living on low state benefits.

However, it is interesting to see that these groups with the lowest median incomes did not appear to be over-represented in the lowest income decile, which is characterised by incomes of less than £115 per week. Although they had low, below-median incomes, overall, lone parents and older people were more concentrated in the other low deciles: II, III and IV. The group of people who were concentrated in decile I were young single people. A substantial proportion, almost one quarter, of young single people aged under 35 were in decile I with the very lowest incomes of all family types. However, although young single people were characterised by some of the lowest incomes, a significant proportion actually had very high incomes and young single people were only slightly under-represented in the top income decile 10: 9 per cent of young single people had incomes of over £650 per week.

These findings of very low and of very high incomes clearly pinpoint substantial heterogeneity within the young single lifecycle cluster. Such heterogeneity is related to the rather wide range of people encompassed within this lifecycle type. 'Single people aged under 35' no doubt consists of unemployed people and those in their first, low paid posts as well as students often combining low paid work with a grant or parental support. This group will also contain those who are in their late twenties and thirties and who have firmly established themselves in good, very well paid jobs in the labour market.

DIFFERENT TYPES OF INCOME

Income can come from a number of possible sources. For this analysis, the source of income has been simplified into five mutually-exclusive income types. These are:

- work-related income
- state benefits
- income from occupational pensions
- investment-related income and
- other income (including child maintenance from ex-partners, educational grants, private benefits and odd jobs).

Table 2.5 gives summary information about these different sources of income. For example, work-related income accounts for a mean of £231 per week, the equivalent of 68 per cent of all income. As mentioned before, however, the mean is affected by the relatively small number of people who have large amounts of income and so, as well as looking at the overall distribution of income, it is helpful to calculate more typical distributions of different types of income. Thus the final column of the table looks at the 'typical portfolio' of income and shows that, on average, work-related income only accounts for 49 per cent of all income. This figure was calculated by looking at the composition of income for each family and then taking the average across all families. Another way of thinking about this is that a typical family received about half of their income in the form of work-related income. Income from state benefits is much more prominent in the typical portfolio than it is in the overall distribution because it is a fairly widespread form of income even though it is fairly small in value. In other words, a typical family received about 37 per cent of their income in the form of benefit income but, overall, benefit income only accounted for about 19 per cent of all income.

Elsewhere in this book, unless otherwise stated, where income or wealth are de-composed into their constituent parts, it is the typical portfolio measure which is being referred to rather than the overall distribution. This is because this measure gives a better indication of the typical breakdown of income or wealth as it is less affected by small numbers of families with very large amounts of income or wealth.

Table 2.5   Sources of income – summary table

	Mean gross income £ per week	Overall distribution of income column %	Typical portfolio column %
Work-related	231	68	49
State benefits	66	19	37
Occupational pension	24	7	7
Investment	14	4	4
Other	6	2	3
Total	341	100	100

Source: 1995/6 *Family Resources Survey*

Table 2.6 confirms the picture emerging from Table 2.5 as there is a link between levels of income and source of income: families with higher levels of income were associated with the dominance of work-related income and families with lower levels of income were associated with the dominance of state benefits. For example, the lifecycle group characterised by the highest income levels – young childless couples – stood out in that the vast majority of their income came from work (Table 2.6). On average, 92 per cent of the total income of young childless couples was work-related. Further, only 5 per cent of this group's income came from state benefits – the lowest share of all lifecycle groups. This goes some way to confirming our earlier suggestion that it is likely that this group of younger couples with no dependent children consists of two workers.

After work-related income, income from state benefits accounted for, on average, the next highest share of total income for the families in the sample, but the proportion of income due to state benefits rose for lower income families. Looking at the lowest income group of lone parents, 69 percent of their income was from the state and only 22 per cent was work-related. This figure of 69 per cent represented one of the highest shares of income from state benefits for all lifecycle groups. However, it is important to note that talking about lone parents serves to make neutral the markedly gendered low income of this lifecycle group. That is, for 91 per cent of the group, 'lone parent' actually means 'lone mother'. Thus, it is women bringing up children on their

Table 2.6 Typical portfolios and overall distributions of income by lifecycle group

	Young singles	Older singles	Young childless couples	Lone parents	Young couples, young children	Older couples, young children	Couples, school-age children	Older childless couples	Pensioner couples	Single pensioners	All
Typical portfolio (column percentages)											
Work-related	66	47	92	22	76	81	79	68	5	1	49
Investment-related	3	5	1	1	1	2	2	4	9	6	4
State benefits	22	39	5	69	21	14	16	17	62	77	37
Occupational pension	0	7	0	0	0	0	1	11	24	15	7
Other	10	1	2	8	1	2	3	0	0	0	3
Overall distribution (column percentages)											
Work-related	86	68	96	36	87	87	87	79	9	4	68
Investment-related	1	5	1	1	1	1	2	5	13	9	4
State benefits	9	19	2	54	10	10	8	7	48	66	19
Occupational pension	0	7	0	1	0	0	1	8	30	21	7
Other	5	1	1	8	1	1	2	0	0	0	2

Source: 1995/6 *Family Resources Survey*

Table 2.7 Gross weekly income levels and typical portfolios for
lone mothers and fathers

	All lone parents	Lone mothers	Lone fathers
Income in £s:			
Median income	165	164	204
Mean income	206	197	293
% of which is, on average:		*Column per cent*	
Work-related	22	20	45
Occupational pension	0	0	1
State benefits	69	72	45
Investment-related	1	0	1
Other	8	8	7
N	2,029	1,837	192

own who, in the absence of a male partner, are characterised by
very low levels of income and by massive reliance on the state for
support. A small minority of lone parents were men, amounting to
192 families in the FRS sample. Lone fathers were experiencing
income disadvantage in that almost half (45 per cent) of their
income was from state benefits, but the corresponding, higher
figure for lone mothers was 72 per cent and lone mothers' income
was even lower than that of lone fathers – at a median of £164 per
week compared with £204 for lone fathers (Table 2.7).

Women also dominated the lifecycle group with the second
lowest income levels: 72 per cent of the single pensioner group
(whose median income stood at a low £181 per week) were
women. This group of single older people were distinctive in that
they were the group for which state benefits accounted for the
highest proportions of total income (77 per cent). However, there
was an added gender disadvantage – the proportions of state
income stood even higher for women (80 per cent) than for men
(71 per cent). Most of the remaining income of single pensioners
came from occupational pensions.

Among those of working age, the group with the second
highest dependence on state benefits (after lone parents) was
single people aged 35–64 without dependent children (see Table
2.6). This is a little surprising, and perhaps even worrying, given

that this group should be in their peak earning years. But it probably reflects the fact that some in this group are early-retired and some are on disability benefits. Older childless couples of the same age group were much less likely to have income from state benefits.

A minority of income (14 per cent of total income) came from sources other than employment or state benefits. Retired people were characterised by having above average shares of investment-related income (see Table 2.6). However, it must be noted that this does not indicate that older people were living comfortably off investments accumulated over their life-times. Investments were bringing in a higher proportion of income for older people, but total income for retired people was still very low. For example, as median income for couple pensioners was only £194 per week, investment income was amounting to only about £17 per week for the whole family. In the main, pensioners were living off a combination of state benefits and, to a lower extent, occupational pensions. The dominance of state benefits and the low levels of state pension in the UK account for their very low income levels.

The remaining forms of income (occupational pension and 'other') made only a 10 per cent contribution to overall income levels for families in the sample. Occupational pensions began to make an impact as families approached the age of 65. This is due to the fact that most women will have retired before 65 and many of the men will be taking early retirement. However, 'other' income in the form of educational grants, maintenance or odd jobs only made a mark for young single people and for lone parents, accounting for about one tenth of each of their total incomes.

WEALTH AND THE LIFECYCLE

Median total assets of families in Britain in 1995/6 stood at just over £53,000. When calculating total assets, we have included financial savings, state pension wealth accumulated to date, private pension wealth (that is, occupational or personal pension wealth) accumulated to date and net housing wealth (see Appendix B for full details of how wealth was measured). The inclusion of state pension wealth may seem surprising given that, unlike the other forms of wealth, people have little choice about paying into the state pension, but state pension wealth is a 'functional equivalent' of private pension wealth and, as our analysis will demonstrate, it is an important source of wealth (indeed, provides the bulk of wealth for some groups). Where appropriate (and in Chapter 5 in particular), we separate out state and private pension wealth. But, unless otherwise stated, 'total wealth' figures include state pension wealth. Unlike income, wealth has not been equivalised to take into account family size. This is because it is not standard practice to equivalise wealth and there has been very little conceptual or empirical work carried out into this issue.

It should be remembered that our 'total wealth' figure includes very diverse forms of wealth: from very liquid forms (such as money in savings accounts) to less liquid forms (such as housing wealth) to non-liquid forms (such as pension wealth). The merits of combining these into one figure are open to debate but it is important to have a total wealth figure in order to look at the distribution of wealth in the

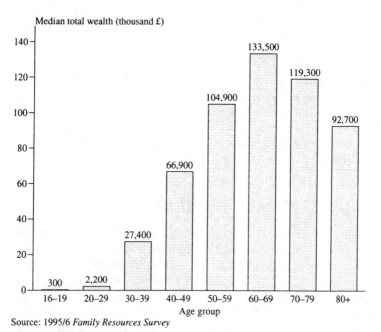

Source: 1995/6 *Family Resources Survey*

Figure 2.3   Median total wealth by age group

same way that we look at the distribution of total income. Otherwise some people who appear rich in terms of housing wealth might actually be rather poor overall because of low levels of financial savings and pension wealth. We need the total picture while remembering the diversity of its component parts.

As with income, the level of assets varied markedly for different age groups and family types (see Table 2.8 which rounds data to two decimal places). Some families were very wealthy indeed. Their wealth served to pull overall mean assets up to over £90,000. On the other hand, some groups had very low, near zero, assets or even negative total wealth. As a result, median total wealth by age group ranged from approximately £300 for 16–19-year-olds to £133,000 for 60–69-year-olds. Wealth increased by age, peaking at 60–69 years and then falling (Table 2.8 and Figure 2.3). Thus we see the classic inverted U or hump shaped distribution of wealth. In this cross-sectional analysis, however, it is not possible to separate age from cohort effects. It may be that these older age groups had lower levels of assets than younger generations in the first place and so it would be cohort/generational effects which would be more important.

Asset levels and lifecycle groups

Being in a couple and being older were both associated with higher wealth. Pensioner couples had the highest levels of wealth of all the lifecycle groups. Total median wealth for these couples was £164,000 (Table 2.9). At a considerable distance behind the retired couples were the older childless couples. As we would expect from lifecycle theory, it is older people without dependent children who have the greatest levels of wealth.

A cluster of families had assets averaging between £50,000 and £100,000. This cluster included, first, older single people with no children, and then single pensioners. These results reinforced the powerful influence of age on families' assets. This cluster of families with high assets (minimum total assets of around £50,000, but who did not have more than £100,000) also included older couples with pre-school age children and couples with children of school age. The uniting feature of these two groups was, potentially, the age of the families. Older couples with pre-school age children are partly defined by the fact that the female partner is aged over 35. Couples with school-age children have

Table 2.8 Total wealth by age group (including financial savings, state and private pension wealth and net housing wealth)

| | Age of head of family | | | | | | | | |
	16–19	*20–29*	*30–39*	*40–49*	*50–59*	*60–69*	*70–79*	*80+*	*All*
Median wealth	300	2,200	27,400	66,900	104,900	133,500	119,300	92,700	53,300
Mean wealth	900	10,800	41,300	86,100	139,700	181,00	161,000	127,900	91,100
N	1,223	5,741	5,780	5,031	4,134	3,937	3,689	1,952	31,487
Row per cent	4	18	18	16	13	13	12	6	100

Table 2.9 Total wealth by lifecycle group (including financial savings, state and private pension wealth and net housing wealth)

| £s | Lifecycle group | | | | | | | | | | |
	Young singles	*Older singles*	*Young childless couples*	*Lone parents*	*Young couples, young children*	*Older couples, young children*	*Couples, school-age children*	*Older childless couples*	*Pensioner couples*	*Single pensioners*	*All*
Median wealth	1,500	49,900	20,000	4,000	28,000	66,200	75,300	114,500	163,900	85,100	53,300
Mean wealth	7,600	79,800	29,000	23,900	39,400	87,200	96,400	155,900	226,100	114,000	91,100
N	5,240	3,837	1,335	2,033	2,327	872	3,309	4,753	3,029	4,570	31,485
Row per cent	17	12	4	7	7	3	11	15	10	15	100

Source for both tables: 1995/6 *Family Resources Survey*

Table 2.10 Wealth deciles by lifecycle group

Column percentages	Young singles	Older singles	Young childless couples	Lone parents	Young couples, young children	Older couples, young children	Couples, school-age children	Older childless couples	Pensioner couples	Single pensioners	All
						Lifecycle group					
Poorest (decile I)	43	2	4	21	4	1	1	1	0	2	10
Deciles II–IX	57	92	95	78	95	93	92	78	65	88	80
Richest (decile X)	0	7	1	1	1	6	8	21	35	10	10

Source: 1995/6 *Family Resources Survey*

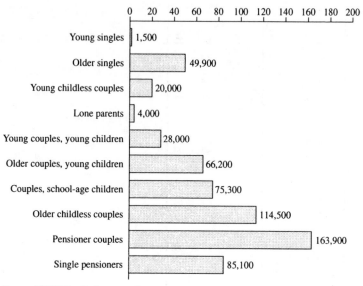

Source: 1995/6 *Family Resources Survey*

Figure 2.4   Median total wealth by lifecycle groups (including housing, financial, state and private pension wealth) (thousand £)

older dependent children and are likely to have slightly older parents than the young couples with pre-school age children. Furthermore, both these groups are likely to be at the stage in life where they are building up their assets. They may well be accumulating pension wealth through work, buying a house and putting money into some form of savings account. The higher incomes of these two groups will support them in this asset-building phase (see later).

As with the income investigation, assets were divided into decile bands to allow us to clarify which lifecycle groups were characterised by extreme wealth, for example, and which groups were concentrated at the very bottom ends of the asset distribution (Table 2.10 and Figure 2.4). The results confirm that wealth is more unequally distributed than is income: it is more concentrated in certain family types. Notably, it seems that wealth is more clearly related to lifecycle positions than is income. For example, unlike the income distributions, variation in wealth *within* lifecycle groups was less extreme. There were no lifecycle groups having significant proportions of families owning very high values of assets, while at the same time having significant proportions of families owning the very lowest levels of assets.

The decile analysis served to reinforce the conclusions made so far: the vast majority of families were in deciles 2–9, but this varied substantially by lifecycle. The groups over-represented in the top wealth decile – with assets of over £200,000 – were pensioner couples and older childless couples. Over a third of pensioner couples were in the richest wealth decile (decile 10) as were one fifth of older childless couples.

The lifecycle groups which stood out as having very little wealth were the young single childless people and lone parents. Both of these lifecycle groups had assets totalling under £4,000 (Table 2.9). The young single people, for example, had a median total of £1,500. The analysis of decile groups (Table 2.10) also shows that the group with the very least wealth (with assets amounting to under £1,200) were young single people. In fact, almost a half of young single people were in the lowest decile and none at all had assets in the top decile band (over £21,000). A fifth of lone parents were also concentrated here, at the bottom of the asset distribution.

The low wealth of young single people will be due to a number of influences mostly reflecting lifecycle effects. First, because of their age, young people will simply have had less time to build up their assets than older groups but may well build up substantial assets in the future. The nature of the measure of assets in this quantitative analysis is that it demonstrates what assets families have accumulated to date, not what their predicted life-time wealth will be. Lower assets for some young people will also be due to their very low incomes and while this can also be partly explained by lifecycle effects, the heterogeneity of incomes within this group suggests that other factors are also at work.

Age cannot explain the low level of assets of lone parents, as most lone parents are not young single mothers but older women who are divorced, widowed or separated. In fact about two-fifths of lone parents were aged between 30 and 39 and a further one fifth were aged 40 to 49. Other factors such as gender and poor employment opportunities are probably more important.

It would seem that low levels of wealth for other lifecycle groups are less to do with their low levels of income but are actually

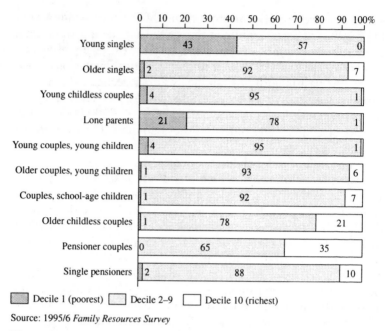

Decile 1 (poorest) ☐ Decile 2–9 ☐ Decile 10 (richest)

Source: 1995/6 *Family Resources Survey*

Figure 2.5   Wealth deciles by lifecycle groups

more to do with their being in the process of building up their assets. young childless couples, for example, have little wealth. However, we know that this group had very high incomes. So, at this stage in their lives, high income young childless couples are probably on the path to high levels of assets in later life. Similarly, young couples with pre-school age children and who have low levels of wealth are likely to be in this 'asset building' phase.

A MATRIX OF THE INCOME AND WEALTH DISTRIBUTION

Previous research has shown that there are direct links between income and wealth with those on high incomes also owning large amounts of wealth (Banks, Dilnot and Low, 1994) but there are some groups who are 'income poor, asset rich' and 'income rich, asset poor'. This section explores the direct links between income and wealth and identifies which lifecycle groups have different combinations of income and wealth.

Median levels of wealth rise as we move up the annual income bands in Table 2.11. Families in the lowest income band, £1–5,000 per year, had median assets of approximately £2,800. However there was large variation within this group as indicated by the higher mean of approximately £32,000. There was a big jump to wealth of about £50,000 for those with income of £5,000–10,000 and a smaller additional jump to wealth levels of £60,000 for those on incomes of £10,000–35,000. The very highest income bands had wealth amounting to over £110,000 (the table (Table 2.12) of median wealth by income deciles reveals a similar picture of high wealth for those with higher incomes).

In the main, higher levels of income were associated with higher levels of wealth and those with little wealth were likely to have low incomes too. However, certain groups fell outside these 'wealth rich, income rich' and 'wealth poor, income poor' typologies. The aim here is to identify which groups fall into the different cells of an income/asset matrix. Families were divided into 'income poor' and 'income rich' families by splitting up those with incomes below the median income and those with incomes equal to or higher than the median. Wealth rich and wealth poor groups were created in a similar way. The resulting four groups were combined to create the income/asset matrix.

Table 2.13 presents various aspects of this analysis. It is based on median wealth of £53,000 and median gross income of £260 per week. Thus it shows four different groups depending on whether families within the group have income and wealth above or below those levels. For example, if we take the 'wealth rich/income rich' group, the table shows that 28 per cent of families fit into this group; that is, they have higher than average wealth and higher than average income. The table then shows that the average (median) wealth of this group was £135,000 and they had weekly gross incomes of £449. Table 2.13 also shows that older childless couples are among three groups who are most likely to fit into this group, with 59 per cent of older childless couples being wealth rich/income rich.

At the other extreme, the 'dual poor' group had average assets of under £6,000 and incomes of about £150 per week. Lone parents were particularly likely to fit into this group.

As just mentioned, the main group of families who fell into the 'dual rich' high income/high wealth band were older childless

Table 2.11 Average total wealth by annual gross income bands

| | Gross annual income | | | | | | | | |
	1–5,000	*5,001– 10,000*	*10,001– 15,000*	*15,001– 20,000*	*20,001– 25,000*	*25,001– 30,000*	*30,001– 35,000*	*35,001– 40,000*	*40,000+*
Mean	31,900	61,800	86,000	95,300	98,900	108,800	117,500	140,700	229,200
Median	2,800	47,200	58,800	58,400	58,200	61,900	64,500	80,700	111,000
N	1,453	9,400	6,025	4,351	3,167	2,181	1,455	913	1,915

Source: 1995/6 *Family Resources Survey*

Table 2.12 Average total wealth by income deciles

| | Income deciles | | | | | | | | | |
	1	*2*	*3*	*4*	*5*	*6*	*7*	*8*	*9*	*10*
Wealth										
Mean	40,700	59,300	61,400	73,100	85,800	93,700	96,900	99,375	112,031	193,577
Median	7,200	46,000	46,900	53,900	58,200	60,600	60,100	58,302	63,177	94,099

Source: 1995/6 *Family Resources Survey*

Table 2.13   A matrix of the income and asset distribution (total percentages). Median wealth and incomes. Lifecycle groups most likely to fit in each cell

Wealth rich/Income rich (28%)	*Wealth rich/Income poor (22%)*
Wealth – £135,500: Income – £449 Older childless couples (59%) Couples with school-age children (49%) Older couples with young children (45%)	Wealth – £109,800: Income – £168 Couple pensioners (67%) Single pensioners (53%)
Wealth poor/Income rich (22%)	*Wealth poor/Income poor (28%)*
Wealth – £14,500: Income – £422 Young childless couples (73%) Young single people (50%)	Wealth – £5,600: Income – £152 Lone parents (75%) Young single people (47%)

Source: 1995/6 *Family Resources Survey*

couples. Fifty-nine per cent of this lifecycle group was above average on both counts. Therefore, older, high-income families have higher assets. Couples with school-age children and older couples with pre-school age children were also found in this band. About half of the older families with children had high incomes and a great deal of wealth.

As we might expect, wealth rich but income poor groups were dominated by pensioners – both those in couples and those on their own. Families located in this cell of the matrix owned assets worth, on average, over £100,000, but their median income was under £200 per week. These groups will no doubt be living on their pensions, on the whole, but will have built up substantial assets.

Wealth poor/income rich groups were characterised by an average wealth level of under £15,000 but by incomes of over £400. Families most likely to be asset poor but income rich were the young childless couples, and also to a lesser extent young single people. We saw above that young couples without any dependent children were likely to be dual earners who, due to their young ages, had not yet had time to build up ample levels of assets. Young single people at the older end of the age band of

Table 2.14 Typical portfolios of income and asset groups (column percentages)

	Asset rich/ Income rich	Asset rich/ Income poor	Asset poor/ Income rich	Asset poor/ Income poor
Work	68	15	91	25
Occupational pension	14	15	0	0
State benefits	12	64	7	66
Investment	6	6	1	2
Other	1	1	2	8

Source: 1995/6 *Family Resources Survey*

their lifecycle group in their early thirties who had well-paid jobs would also be in this asset-building stage.

Finally, the group which was conspicuous in having low amounts of wealth (under £6,000) and living on low incomes (under £200) was lone parents. Although young, single people were also likely to be income and asset poor, as predicted from the above analyses, lone parents emerged as the group with combined lowest income and lowest wealth. Fully 75 per cent of lone parents had lower than average incomes and lower than average wealth. We know that their lower incomes are due to the dependence of lone mothers on state benefits. If we look at actual asset types, as we do in the next section, it will be shown that, in addition to being very low, lone parents' wealth is of a very particular form; the vast majority of their assets are due to the accumulation of compulsory state pension credits.

Table 2.14 shows that, on average, the major source of income for the income-rich groups is from paid work. The asset poor/income poor group typically receive more of their income through earnings compared with the asset rich/income poor group because the latter group are more likely to have income from occupational pensions and investments.

DIFFERENT TYPES OF WEALTH

Previous research has shown that there is a relationship between levels of wealth and different types of wealth. In other words, people with different levels of assets hold their assets in different ways (McKay, 1992). Those with fewest assets have liquid assets such as savings accounts. Those with 'middling assets' hold them in property and/or pension rights. The 'super-wealthy' own land or shares in businesses (often their own companies). Thus, those with the fewest assets often have the most heavily taxed assets and the assets with the lowest rates of return.

Portfolio composition

This section reviews the combinations, or portfolios, of wealth, which different groups have accumulated. Analysis of the 1995/6 *Family Resources Survey* has calculated accumulated pension wealth to date rather than projecting likely pension wealth over an individual's lifetime up to retirement. This analysis includes both state pension wealth and private pension wealth (by which we mean both occupational and personal pension wealth). Housing wealth has been calculated net of mortgages, so figures give details of housing equity rather than the market value of a property. Appendices A and B gives details of the analysis of both pension and housing wealth.

As we saw in relation to income, there are different ways to break down the composition of wealth. If we take all pension wealth together (including state, occupational and personal pension), it is clear that pension wealth took the largest share of all wealth, with about half of all wealth being in the form of pension wealth (see Table 2.15). This figure for pension wealth breaks down into 26 per cent for state pension assets and 22 per cent for private pension assets. Housing wealth then accounted for just over a third of all wealth and financial wealth accounted for 17 per cent. If we exclude state pension wealth (as most analyses of wealth usually do) then housing wealth dominates (see Table 2.15).

Table 2.15 also looks at the typical portfolio of different types of wealth (see page 28 for further explanation of this measure) and shows that 62 per cent of wealth is 'typically' held in pension assets (this breaks down into 49 per cent in state pension assets and 14 per cent in private pension assets). The overall distribution gives less weight to pension wealth because, as we shall see in Chapter 4, in comparison with other forms of wealth, state pension

Table 2.15 Different types of wealth – summary table

	Mean levels £	Overall distribution Column percentages	Typical portfolio Column percentages	Overall distribution (excluding state pension)
State pension wealth	23,900	26	49	
Private pension wealth	19,700	22	14	29
Housing wealth	31,700	35	26	47
Financial wealth	15,800	17	11	24
Total	91,100	100	100	100

Source: 1995/6 *Family Resources Survey*

wealth is very widespread but fairly small in terms of value. Thus although pension wealth will play a vital role for a 'typical family', a few families have very large amounts of money in financial savings and housing and this skews the overall distribution away from pension wealth. The rest of this chapter combines state and private pension wealth, but the two are split out in Chapter 4, when more detail is given about each particular type of wealth.

Two factors help to explain varying compositions of wealth: age and level of wealth. Generally, younger people have had little time to accumulate pension wealth and so have smaller amounts of money in pensions than older people, but because they have such small overall amounts of wealth, pension wealth is a fairly important part of their portfolio. Older people have much larger amounts of pension wealth but the proportion of their wealth in pension wealth is generally smaller because they have much greater total assets (Tables 2.16, 2.17a and 2.17b). An exception to this is retired people who have high amounts of wealth, of which a large proportion is, in fact, due to the pensions they had built up over their working lives.

As a proportion of all wealth, housing wealth is most important for those in middle age for a number of reasons: younger people are less likely to have put their foot on the housing ladder and some older people will have never got on the ladder because their generation would have missed the recent expansion in owner-occupation. Also, older groups will also have very large amounts

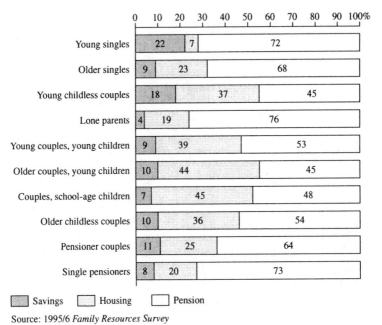

	Savings	Housing	Pension

Source: 1995/6 *Family Resources Survey*

Figure 2.6   Typical portfolios of wealth by lifecycle groups

in pension entitlements which will dwarf even large amounts of housing wealth.

Families with the very lowest levels of assets – young people and lone parents – differed in their asset composition. Compared with young single people, proportionately more of the wealth of lone parents was typically due to housing assets and only a tiny proportion (4 per cent) was in financial savings (see Figure 2.6). This suggests that the group of lone parents consists of those who have been at the house-buying stage in their lives – and perhaps accumulated some housing wealth as the result of a 'clean break settlement' with their ex-partners. We saw earlier that three-fifths of lone parents were aged 30 or more. However, these and other, younger, lone parents either have never had the chance to build up financial assets or, alternatively, have used up this most liquid part of their resources. In times of financial difficulty, savings in bank accounts will no doubt be the first assets to go. They are often the most accessible assets and, in addition, cashing them in represents a less drastic act than does selling a home.

Table 2.16 Typical portfolios of wealth by age (proportions)

Column percentages	Age of head of family								
	16–19	*20–29*	*30–39*	*40–49*	*50–59*	*60–69*	*70–79*	*80+*	*All*
Housing	0	15	34	38	33	25	21	21	26
Pension	77	67	56	53	58	65	70	71	62
Financial	23	18	10	8	9	10	9	9	11

Source: 1995/6 *Family Resources Survey*

Table 2.17a Distribution of wealth by lifecycle group

Column percentages	Lifecycle group									
	Young singles	*Older singles*	*Young childless couples*	*Lone parents*	*Young couples, young children*	*Older couples, young children*	*Couples, school-age children*	*Older childless couples*	*Pensioner couples*	*Single pensioners*
Typical portfolios										
Housing	7	23	37	19	39	44	45	36	25	20
Pension	72	68	45	76	53	45	48	54	64	73
Financial	22	9	18	4	9	10	7	10	11	8
Overall distribution										
Housing	38	33	49	54	57	51	52	36	25	26
Pension	33	51	27	39	29	29	35	46	54	58
Financial	30	16	25	7	19	19	13	18	21	15

Source: 1995/6 *Family Resources Survey*

Table 2.17b Levels of wealth by lifecycle group

Column percentages		Young singles	Older singles	Young childless couples	Lone parents	Young couples, young children	Older couples, young children	Couples, school-age children	Older childless couples	Pensioner couples	Single pensioners
							Lifecycle group				
Levels of:											
Housing wealth											
Median		0	0	9,000	0	14,000	37,000	43,800	48,500	59,400	0
Mean		2,900	26,300	14,100	13,000	22,500	44,800	50,500	56,700	56,900	29,800
Pension wealth											
Median		1,000	27,100	4,600	3,200	6,670	17,500	22,200	48,400	95,600	53,200
Mean		2,500	40,800	7,700	9,400	11,500	25,700	33,400	71,900	121,300	66,500
Financial wealth											
Median		0	300	1,400	0	300	1,600	900	3400	6,200	1,500
Mean		2,300	12,700	7,200	1,600	5,500	16,800	12,500	27,300	47,900	17,600

Source: 1995/6 *Family Resources Survey*

The asset profile was reversed for the young single people. Apart from pension wealth, most of their wealth was, on average, in the form of financial savings or investments. A number of possible interpretations arise for the situation of the younger single life-cycle group. It may be that, at this stage, very few people are able to invest in housing. Or, it may be that young people have less interest in buying a house, prefer to be more mobile and to have quicker access to their assets. However, the low incomes of some of these younger people tend to support the first interpretation. It suggests that, even if they wanted to buy a house, young people would be deterred from entering the housing market due to low income. Related to their low incomes and also to the general insecurity in the labour market for young people (Pollock, 1997; Roberts, 1984), young people may be wary of making the long term commitment which is associated with a mortgage.

If we look now at some of the families with higher levels of assets, two groups stand out as having larger shares of their wealth in housing. On average, housing assets play an important role for older couples with pre-school age children and couples with school-age children and accounts for almost half of the total assets of these two groups.

So far we have concentrated on typical portfolios. Table 2.17a also shows the overall distribution of wealth and it is clear from this table that, although pension wealth is widespread it is a far less important source of wealth in overall value terms. For example, lone parents typically have 76 per cent of their wealth in the form of pension wealth but, overall, only 39 per cent of the wealth of lone parents is accounted for by pension wealth. In value terms, housing wealth is the dominant form of wealth for lone parents overall. This means that a small group of lone parents have substantial amounts of housing wealth as a proportion of their total wealth.

It is clear from all of this analysis that not only are levels of wealth related to lifecycle (as we saw earlier), but that the dominant form of wealth also differs between lifecycle groups.

The different types of wealth of the income/asset groups

Table 2.18 shows that families who are asset rich, whether or not they have high incomes, have, on average, more of their wealth in the form of housing than do families which are asset poor. In the sample, families with most of their wealth located in pensions were those with low assets and low incomes. So, the lower the level of total assets, the more likely they are to be in pension form. However, it also appears that groups with low assets but higher incomes have less of their overall assets in pension form than families with low assets who live on below average incomes.

Table 2.18   Income and wealth combinations by level of wealth and typical portfolio of asset

	Wealth rich/ income rich	*Wealth rich/ income poor*	*Wealth poor/ income rich*	*Wealth poor/ income poor*
Median assets (£)	135,500	109,800	14,500	5,600
On average, of which %				
Housing	43	37	18	8
Financial	13	7	17	9
Pension	44	56	65	83

Source: 1995/6 *Family Resources Survey*

3
—

Knowledge and Views about Wealth

In Chapter 2, analysis of the 1995/6 *Family Resources Survey* showed that there were clear links between income, wealth and the lifecycle: high income groups generally had high levels of wealth and this was related to lifecycle position – for example, older childless couples generally had high levels of both income and wealth. At the other end of the spectrum, lone parents had low levels of both income and wealth. In this chapter, we begin to seek an explanation for the links between income, wealth and the lifecycle by drawing on the qualitative research. The qualitative research involved 40 in-depth interviews (see Appendices C and D for further details). Such a sample size means that the research is not representative of wider views but does give an indication of the range and type of views which might occur more widely.

KNOWLEDGE ABOUT ASSETS

In this section, we discuss knowledge of the existence of different methods of saving and investment (including financial savings, pensions and mortgages) and the way in which they operate. We also explore the extent to which different levels of knowledge can explain different levels of asset accumulation and we show that high levels of knowledge do not, in themselves, lead to greater asset-accumulation. If anything, the relationship is in reverse, with the ability to accumulate assets leading to the acquisition of greater knowledge about saving and investments. Along with ability to accumulate assets, levels of knowledge can also be explained by other factors such as social class, gender, age and lifecycle stage.

Levels of knowledge were classified on the basis of *awareness* of the availability of different options for saving and investing money and *understanding* of what each method involved. The levels of awareness and understanding associated with different levels of knowledge were as follows:

'High'
- awareness of a wide range of methods of saving and investing money
- at least some understanding of the detail involved in these methods
- evidence of an informed choice in terms of their own methods of saving and investing money.

'Medium'
- either, a detailed understanding of their own methods of saving and investment but not a wider understanding of the available options
- or, a broad awareness of a wide range of methods of saving and investment but little detailed understanding of any of them.

'Low'
- little awareness of the range of methods available for saving and investing money
- low levels of understanding of their own savings/investments.

The terms 'high', 'medium' and 'low' are not being used here in any absolute sense but in a relative sense – as a way of comparing people in different groups. It is interesting to note, however, that those whom we classified as having a high level of knowledge perceived themselves as having a relatively low level of knowledge. The more detail that people uncovered about different methods of saving and investment, the more they recognised the complexities of the personal finance market. One man in his 40s, who had a fairly clear and accurate understanding of savings and investment products, described his level of understanding as that of a 'layman'. He ascribed this partly, however, to the fact that financial markets were subject to perpetually changing influences which made it difficult to feel certain about the detail of any products. He remarked:

> *One never knows... I was happy enough at the time... [but] I suppose knowing that governments are going to change, interest rates are going to change, all those sorts of things.*

Consequently, the more people knew, the more likely they were to identify gaps in their knowledge which, to a degree, undermined their confidence in their own ability to make judgements in this area.

The analysis presented below suggests that levels and patterns of knowledge about methods of saving and investment were largely explained by factors such as lifecycle group, income, social class, gender, and experience of different types of saving and investment products.

Lifecycle stage, age and trigger events

Levels of knowledge were influenced, to a large degree, by age and stage in the lifecycle. Middle-aged couples without dependent children were better informed about savings and investments than those at other lifecycle stages. Young people and families with children had slightly lower levels of knowledge. Nonetheless, some people clearly had developed at least medium, and sometimes even high, levels of knowledge while still at an early stage in their lives. Surprisingly, perhaps, pensioners also had relatively low levels of knowledge. This could be because they never developed the necessary knowledge, or because levels of awareness and understanding fall as people get older. There may also be cohort effects at work here with some aspects of saving, such as mortgage endowment policies, being relatively new and so of less relevance to people in their 70s and 80s.

Some people with high levels of knowledge about saving and investment had experienced trigger factors which had necessitated seeking information on saving and investment. For example, 'nesting', by which we primarily mean finding a long-term a partner and setting up a home, was a significant trigger in information-seeking about saving and investment. A man in his early 20s, working in service sector management had recently bought a house with his fiancée, also in her early 20s. He had begun to think about all of the things he wanted to do in the future, including getting married and having a family, and this had made him realise how important it was to have financial security. He explained:

> ... *as you get older you do start to think about buying a house, buying a car, you know, you take your first loan out to buy a car.*

> *I don't know, you just realise that you're going to need money a lot more in the future... You need more security in your life, so you have to save.*

Setting up home with his fiancée had prompted him to find out what methods of saving and investing money were available and he was keen to find ways of saving which would offer him good returns as well as security in the long-term. This necessitated going beyond the basic savings accounts which his bank or building society could offer.

Redundancy was also an important trigger for some people because they had to work out the best way to cope with the associated loss of income and disruption to the household. Also, people who received redundancy settlements were very likely to seek advice on the best way to manage a lump-sum payment.

As mentioned above, many people with low knowledge were young, with little money to spare and were not thinking seriously about saving. Few were earning high salaries or wages and, therefore, were rarely, if ever, left with money to save at the end of the week or month. In addition, many had not been in employment for long and were still enjoying the freedom of having their own income to spend as they pleased. Also, most were in their very early 20s and none were married or in a serious relationship. Consequently, they had not started to think about 'settling down', which was an important explanation for high levels of knowledge among some groups of young people.

Older people with low levels of knowledge were also at a stage in their lives when their perceived needs for information were relatively low. They were not actively saving money in any form, they had paid off mortgages and were in the process of running down their pension entitlement and any financial savings they had accrued. Consequently, they felt that they needed very little, if any, information on savings and investment and were not seeking any.

Income and social class

As just discussed, there was an interaction between lifecycle stage, income and levels of knowledge. For example, young people were generally on low incomes and so felt little need for knowledge about saving because their ability to save was limited. Within particular lifecycle groups, however, income varied and where income was high, knowledge about savings was also higher than it was among those on lower incomes.

Social class was also a factor – people from higher social classes (AB in particular) often, although not always, had higher levels of knowledge than people of other social classes. In many cases, social class was linked to literacy and numeracy and people with a high level of knowledge were clearly not daunted by figures or financial information in the field of savings and investments. Those in this group were also often part of a social or professional circle of people who were relatively wealthy and were interested in methods of saving and investment. Consequently, the field of personal finance was more of a 'known quantity' to them. In fact, several people had developed a strong awareness and understanding of savings and investments from working in an environment in which dealing with figures and money had been the norm. For example, a couple in their 70s had a very sophisticated knowledge of a whole range of savings and investment options. The husband, a retired factory manager, had been responsible for managing spending and budgets. His wife had previously been married to a bank manager and she had discussed their joint financial affairs with him.

More important, however, was the fact that everyone who had a high level of knowledge had sufficient income to be actively saving at the time of the research, not for specifics, but more generally for 'the future'. This had heightened both their awareness of the need to develop an understanding of the available options and their concern to invest as effectively as possible in order to receive the maximum return on their money. So high levels of knowledge about savings did not lead to asset-accumulation – an ability to accumulate assets led to high levels of knowledge being developed.

It is not altogether surprising that the savings and investment portfolios of people with lower levels of knowledge tended to be as basic as their understanding. Bank and building society savings accounts were clearly the main focus of saving among these people. They differed from those with high levels of knowledge in both their approach to learning about personal finance and the context in which they did so. None of the respondents who came into this category lived or worked in an environment in which figures and financial information played a large role. Neither had they experienced any trigger events which had raised the profile of financial information in their lives. Consequently, they acquired information in a very pragmatic and incremental way, operating very much on a 'need to know' basis. One young woman, married and in her late 20s explained:

> *Just what I need to know about really... That's all, I'm quite ignorant actually to some things, but it's just what [I need] at the time, you know.*

They often consciously restricted the amount of information they obtained because they were daunted by an over-abundance of detail which only made decision-making more complicated. One widow in her 70s explained:

> *I haven't read a great deal about it, not really. I just take things on face value... I don't go into it at all. It gets too complicated for my simple mind.*

Consequently, no one in this group felt that they lacked information. People with lower levels of knowledge mostly perceived themselves to be 'ordinary' people with little money to invest and, therefore, saving and investments had a very limited role to play in their lives. One elderly woman living alone remarked '*I'm not a financial wizard. I haven't got the money to be that way, so it doesn't matter, does it?* Consequently, they were not overly interested in the minutiae of personal finance and were, in addition, sceptical about the value of adding endless detail to the information they had on savings and investment. They had very little money to worry about and certainly were not thinking about initiating any new methods of saving or investment. One couple in their 80s said '*Our little bit isn't worth much anyway. At our age, it's just there for when we die...*'. Another elderly couple remarked: '*No, we're happy as we are... if we had a lot of money, then we'd probably put it in shares or something. But, I mean, our little bit...*' More importantly, they said that they reached information overload very quickly and this was an important disincentive to seek additional information. A widow in her early 60s whose husband had taken control of financial decisions when they were married, explained:

> *Sometimes I can get a bit, you know, when you read it and you think... 'does this apply to me?' The mind boggles and you don't know what does apply to you. You can get a bit confused sometimes, how they put it – in the jargon, they put it... By the time you've read, 'if this and if that and if the other', you're just back to square one again.*

Gender

Although it is difficult to ascertain whether gender has an effect on real levels of knowledge about savings and investment, gender differences were apparent in the way in which men and women *talked about* their understanding. Men tended to be more confident about their knowledge than women, who were cautious about saying they had a good understanding, despite being able to demonstrate a good grasp of a wide range of saving and investment products. While men were willing to concede that their knowledge was not totally comprehensive, they were far more likely than women to dismiss gaps in their understanding as 'detail rather than substance'. In addition, women were far more likely than men to admit to feeling that they needed further information. Finally, men relished 'shopping around' for information far more than women, who were more likely to express a need for more specific information relating to their own circumstances, than simply to seek more information on a general level.

INFORMATION-SEEKING AND SOURCES OF ADVICE

Another important issue raised in the in-depth interviews was how people differed in their approaches to information-seeking and usage of different sources. For example, a common factor among those with a high level of knowledge was a recognition and acceptance of the need to 'shop around' for financial products to ensure that they had a well-rounded perspective. A retired man in his early 70s commented:

> *I think you've got to be [proactive]. If you're not proactive then you don't get the information. People put money in the savings accounts, and that's still there, and they've been there twenty years and they're getting about 2 or 3 per cent interest on them. You've got to watch these things...*

Consequently, people in this group were the only ones to seek information actively, rather than simply absorb mass-produced information. They sought out information relating specifically to their own needs in newspapers and other published sources, but also on the Internet and teletext and on a one-to-one basis from advisers, colleagues, friends and family. Those with only a low or medium level of knowledge, by contrast, drew on more general sources of published information. They read the finance pages of their regular newspaper, leaflets, mailshots, bill-board, TV and radio advertising.

Much of the difference in information-seeking was related to social class. People from social classes A or B were more likely than anyone else, regardless of their level of knowledge about saving and investment, to have benefitted from personal advice about savings and investments. In part, this was from professional advisors. However, it was more often the result of social interaction with family, friends, colleagues and employers who had similar financial circumstances and were willing to engage in discussions about money. Indeed, several people from class A or B had friends who were financial advisers. Many others had had a financial adviser recommended to them from others within their social circle or family.

Gender was also an important factor. Women often felt themselves to be excluded from these sources of information and advice. They were extremely unlikely to have sought advice from a professional, unless they had experienced a significant trigger event, such as receiving a lump sum in redundancy pay or a large bequest. Further, they knew few other people who had done so. Many felt that they were unlikely to be taken seriously by professional advisers. Sometimes, this was based on experience;

> *To be honest... I found it very, very difficult. But when I took a male friend with me, it was so much easier... Because I found that they would listen to you more. I think being a woman you sort of find it very hard... but as soon as you take a man with you... I can phone up sometimes and it's not always available, but when my sons do it, it's done straight away.*

More often, however, people had not even considered seeking formal financial advice because they perceived their needs to be too 'ordinary' to warrant the attention of a professional. A woman in her 50s, who had taken early retirement from her job in a retail outlet due to ill-health, said;

> *I've heard of financial advisers, I know that, you know, they can guide you into the best way to invest. But... I wouldn't know how to go about contacting one of those, you know. It sounds very daunting...*

The cost of seeking professional financial advice was also prohibitive for many people and several people noted the irony of spending money to seek advice about saving. These feelings became stronger the further along the social class spectrum people were situated.

Mistrust of financial advice

However, regardless of class or gender there was universal confusion about who could be relied on for truly independent advice and most people harboured a deep mistrust of 'advice and sell' situations. Even people who had had contacts with financial advisers were suspicious of them. One young couple who had a good basic level of knowledge about savings and investments outlined their concerns;

The advantage is that they should know what they're talking about. But some of the disadvantages are that they can force their [product] onto you... [S]ome of them are tied to the banks, and they just say 'Well, you've got to have mine', and they make it sound like the best one, and really it mightn't be.

However, this suspicion also applied, to some degree, to advice from banks and building societies, and contained in newspapers, leaflets and mailshots.

In fact, almost everyone expressed a scepticism bordering, in some cases, on insecurity about the actual 'independence' of any source. Many people were deeply confused about where to go for impartial advice, and how to judge whether the advice they received was, in reality, independent. Indeed, some felt that there was no such thing. Consequently, many people spoke of the need to 'cross-check' all financial information and advice. For some, this was a significant barrier to information seeking. One woman recalled the experience of her elderly mother:

> *One of her policies had matured ... and all she wanted to do was to get her money. The guy came in and even though she is an old lady he came in and overwhelmed her and got her signing everything before she knew what she was doing. It was only when this came through the post she found she had tied all her money up in something else – she was absolutely devastated. So I 'phoned them up and gave them some serious aggro because they had conned her ... she got out of it ... but it upset her.*

Although there was near universal suspicion of financial advisers in general, some people had received advice from particular financial advisers whom they trusted.

Information needs

Virtually everyone said that they needed information which was simple, trustworthy and free. Those with little money wanted advice which was tailor-made to their particular situations. As one man said:

> *I'd need somebody to sit down and talk to me about my personal circumstances – somebody to come and talk to me about what I earn, my commitments, spare cash I've got, how it could be invested. If I came into a windfall, what I can do with it, things like that. I don't need general, I need specific.*

There was a widespread view that it would be easy and worthwhile to seek and pay for information if people had a fair amount of money to invest, but that advisers were not geared to the needs of the 'ordinary punter' as one respondent put it or 'the people with only a couple of bob to spare', as another saw it. One commented:

> *If you've got a few thousand to put away ... they're more interested in you and will advise you more. But if you've only got a small amount they don't tend to give you much [advice].*

Although respondents generally felt that they lacked suitable information, they said that they had far too much general and detailed information. 'Information overload' was a problem, particularly because respondents were not particularly interested in financial products and so wanted to know as little as possible. With regard to pensions and mortgages, one respondent said:

> *I want to know exactly how much I'm paying out at the end of the month, that's all I want to know ... I dare say if I wanted more information I would ask!*

ATTITUDES TO SAVING

The previous sections of this chapter sought to explain differences in levels of knowledge about savings and wealth, and to see whether these, in turn, could explain differences in levels of wealth accumulation. The remaining sections now turn to attitudes. They begin by looking at attitudes to saving in general and then consider attitudes towards accumulating housing wealth and pension wealth. The final section considers attitudes to running down these different assets.

This section considers whether attitudes to saving can explain differences in asset accumulation. For example, it could easily be assumed that some people accumulate little wealth because they prefer to spend, so place little importance on saving and investment. As we shall see, however, the picture is much more complex than this and, to a large extent, attitudes towards saving are shaped by ability to accumulate assets rather than vice versa.

Early on in the interviews, respondents were asked to select from a list of three attitudes to saving one statement corresponding most closely with their own. The three statements were:

- You should always try to save money for a rainy day.
- You should save money at some stages in your life but not all the time.
- You should live for the day and not worry about saving for the future.

Overall, people's attitudes to saving divided, almost equally, between the first two options. Very few said that their attitude was one of 'living for the day' but this may be partly because such a statement is less culturally acceptable and so people are reluctant to admit in an interview that they feel this way. In reality, however, people's actual approaches to saving did not necessarily reflect their stated attitude. By no means all of those who felt that saving was always important were able to save money on a regular basis.

Most people in the sample, regardless of their attitudes to saving, were forced to adjust their behaviour in response to other pressures on their finances.

It should be mentioned that sometimes the interviews were carried out with couples, and generally, where both members of a couple were interviewed together, they were in agreement over their attitude to saving. Occasionally, however, individual members of a couple held different views and both viewpoints were explored during the interview. In these circumstances the more cautious member of the couple tended to take responsibility for decision-making around spending and saving money and, at least to a degree, regulate the behaviour of their more 'cavalier' partner.

Other research shows that exploring attitudes is not necessarily the most meaningful route to understanding their behaviour. This is because, while attitudes tend to be stable over time, *beliefs* are subject to change because they are more situation specific (Kempson and Ford, 1995; Whyley *et al*, 1997). Consequently, beliefs, which are continually revised to take the demands of particular situations into account, are much more likely to influence behaviour than general attitudes and may be a more meaningful tool with which to classify behavioural groups. From the in-depth interviews, three distinct approaches to saving money can be identified which approximate to the overall attitudes outlined above but which also incorporate beliefs about saving. The typology is outlined in Table 3.1 overleaf.

Several factors, including lifecycle, level of income and social class explain why people took these different attitudes to saving.

The dedicated savers

Dedicated savers said that they had always thought it important to save at all stages of their lives and so they did not fit neatly into the lifecycle theory of wealth accumulation. Social class was clearly an important element of some, but by no means all, of the *dedicated savers'* approach to saving. This was not due to class conditioning, however, but to the financial circumstances and, more importantly, the stability that they enjoyed. Several of them were in relatively high-status, managerial occupations which afforded high salaries. Consequently, they were better able to

Table 3.1 Typology of approaches to saving

Approach to saving	Characteristics of approach
Dedicated savers	• believe that it is *always* important to save money • focus of saving general, not specific, ie 'for the future' • set aside or 'ring-fence' money to be saved; • expect to save on a regular basis throughout lifetime • are not planning to spend savings until retirement.
Circumstantial savers	• some believed that saving was *always* important but most believed it was only *sometimes* possible • focus of saving specific – car, holidays etc; • save whatever is left after other expenses have been met • plan to spend savings either out of choice or necessity.
Non-savers	• believed in 'living for the day' • not saving anything at all • no plans to start saving in the future • believe money better spent than saved.

afford to save regularly throughout their lives without needing to divert income to other sources. It was therefore ability to save which led to positive attitudes towards saving.

In addition, most of the people in this group were not unduly burdened with other calls on their income. Dedicated savers were least in evidence among people with children and in most cases dedicated savers consisted of dual earners. So, an important basis for understanding the saving behaviour of many dedicated savers was their *ability* to save regularly.

However, not all dedicated savers were middle-class dual-earning couples on high incomes. Further, some other people who were from social classes A and B had a very different attitude to saving. So what does unite all of the dedicated savers to help us to understand why they developed this approach to saving? Three key factors were common to all of the dedicated savers and were central in their adoption of this particular approach to saving money:

- parental influence over attitudes to saving
- marital status
- a quest for a sense of security.

The importance of parental influence was mentioned unfailingly as a key factor in the development of dedicated savers attitudes towards saving money which, in turn, determined their approach. In most cases, dedicated savers' parents had, themselves, held very strict attitudes to saving and been very careful money managers. This had communicated the importance of saving and financial planning to them. Further, dedicated savers' parents had frequently encouraged them to start saving their pocket money from a very young age. This had instilled a discipline of regular saving which had been carried over from childhood into adulthood. Other dedicated savers, however, had developed this attitude to saving because their parents had *not* been careful with money, and they had seen the problems this could cause. It was beyond the scope of this research to explain why some people accept while others reject their parents' approaches to money. Perhaps people merely justify their own opinions with reference to their parents' views, whether these are the same or completely opposite to their own.

Marital status is an interesting element in understanding dedicated savers' approach because not all were in the same position. In part, the influence of marital status was related to lifecycle stage. Among young people without children, dedicated savers were almost all people who had begun 'nesting' and had, consequently, begun to think seriously about their future plans and aspirations. So, as we saw in relation to knowledge, trigger events such as 'nesting' were important in explaining approaches to saving. A young dedicated saver who had recently bought a house with his partner explained:

> *Maybe I'm just quite safe. I don't know... I always want a good life as I get older. You know, I want to have a nice house, I want to have holidays all the time, I want to retire wealthy.*

Being part of a couple clearly engendered a strong sense of responsibility which was a key element of their attitude towards saving. Young people who were not in a cohabiting relationship were far less likely to hold a strict attitude towards saving.

Feeling a sense of responsibility for another individual as well as themselves remained an important incentive to maintain a very strict attitude to saving throughout the lifecycle. It became clearly apparent among older dedicated savers who had had to start considering the implications of poor health and death. One man in his 80s suspected that his wife would need quite a lot of care as she got older. He was determined that, should he be unable to provide that care for her, she would be comfortable and well looked after. He explained:

> ... [I]t's right on my mind at my time of life. Because I used to buy a new car every year, you know, whereas now I've kept this one now for five years... now I find that I think to myself, 'You never know what's happening to you at our time of life' and if anything happened to me I'd like to think that my wife, if she's ever got to go in a residential home, I don't want her to go into a doss house. I want her to go into a posh place, where she's going to be looked after with the same standard as we've had from our own life.

However, it was not simply being part of a couple which was important in holding a strict attitude to saving. A divorced woman in her 50s, who had suddenly found herself having to develop financial independence after her marriage broke down, had also adopted a very strict attitude to saving. Previously her husband had taken control of financial decision-making and he was not predisposed towards strict, regular saving. As soon as she became responsible for the family's finances, she was able to adopt her own approach to saving. Consequently, she described financial independence as, 'Very important. Very important, I don't like to depend on other people, not at all'.

Despite the importance of the factors outlined above in the development of a strict attitude to saving, this final factor was the fundamental unifying factor among all dedicated savers. Although all of them felt financially secure at the time of the research, they were all driven by a sense of insecurity which rendered them unable to relax their attitude towards saving. For some, this was the result of a more general sense of insecurity which pervaded all aspects of their lives. A woman in her 40s explained:

> *I've just never felt secure enough to just go out and spend, from being very young ... I've always had to have money in the bank or the building society – always know that I can cover my bills in case something tragic happened.*

This woman thought that her attitude stemmed from the general insecurity she felt as a child when her family had little money and yet spent what they had quite freely. She believed that she had reacted against her parents' way of approaching money. Most dedicated savers, however, were driven by specific sources of insecurity, often related to lifecycle stage, against which financial savings provided a crucial buffer or safety net. This was, indeed, the way in which savings were perceived among all of the dedicated savers.

Several, predominantly younger, dedicated savers were preoccupied with job insecurity and this uncertainty was their main motivation for prioritising regular saving. One man in his early 20s, working in a managerial occupation, explained:

> *I mean I've seen friends been made redundant at a young age... and they've had nothing, and they've had to start again, and they've had to sell the car because they can't afford the loan anymore. So that's probably the biggest worry, that if I lost my job I'd still be able to keep a good standard of living for a while.*

The desire for security was also particularly strong among people with children and those anticipating starting a family. This, too, provided an important context for attitudes to saving, and putting money aside to secure a stable, comfortable life for a family was a key motivation for adopting a strict attitude to saving. Starting a family can therefore be seen as another important trigger in relation to financial decision-making. One young couple who were thinking of starting a family said:

> *I think when [we] have children or when [we] plan to have children, I'll probably save even more... Again, just the security for them and for ourselves. I wouldn't want them to go without, so I would always want more money for them.*

Feelings of insecurity among older people were of a very different nature and related to their desire to remain independent and, in particular, to avoid 'being a burden' on their children. While most older people in the sample were concerned that they may need to depend on their families for care, they were horrified at the idea of being financially dependent on their adult children. Consequently, financial security was paramount and this was a central element of their attitude towards saving. This desire for independence was not focused just on the rest of their lives, but also the period after their deaths. A couple in their 80s explained:

F: *We've even got our own plot.*
M: *We've bought our headstone.*
F: *I don't want the family to be bothered... my daughter-in-law's family, their parents have just died and, to see them sorting things out, it's so sad. I said to Jack, 'We'll pick our plot, which we have, and pay for the stone and everything', so I've got nothing to worry about like that. I know we can't go together, but at least it's done with. It's awful when anybody dies and you've got to start thinking about a burial and things, isn't it?*

As we have seen, many respondents mentioned greater stability and security as necessary conditions to encourage asset-building. One AB man in his 20s said that job insecurity was discouraging him from saving in particular ways and meant that he was keeping his money in more readily-accessible schemes rather than those which might have better rates of return:

Just the insecurity of a job for everybody now. I mean, I feel mine's really safe, but even so everything's changing so much. That stops me from doing a lot more [saving] especially the risk ones and the long-term [savings/investment schemes] 'cause I'm always worried that myself or my partner could be laid off.

As has been argued by Ulrich Beck (1992), modern society is increasingly becoming a 'risk society' with greater personal and economic uncertainty in people's lives. This was certainly echoed by respondents who felt that such uncertainties were having a major impact on financial attitudes and behaviour. One man in his 60s commented:

When I was young, you could look forward to whatever life you've got with a relative sort of [security]. But now, I mean, it's gone so chaotic, I mean, talking to the lads at work, they don't bother about the future because it might not be there! ... They don't seem to be at all concerned, that's why they grab it and spend and have a good time.

The influence of these three factors – parental influence, marital status and the desire for security – combined to ensure that attitudes to saving among people in this group were an integral part of their personality. They were prepared to exercise financial constraint in the short-term in order to achieve security and stability in the long-term. Consequently, dedicated savers felt that they were unlikely to change their attitude to saving money, at least until retirement.

Circumstantial savers

Unlike the dedicated savers, the *circumstantial savers* conformed quite closely to the lifecycle theory in that they believed that there would be stages in their lives when strict saving was necessary, coupled with periods during which regular saving was either inappropriate or impossible. They differed from dedicated savers in two respects. First, while the vast majority of dedicated savers were saving for general purposes (such as retirement or 'a rainy day'), circumstantial savers were saving for specific items of expenditure which they simply could not otherwise afford. Consequently, they tended to spend their money as soon as they had accrued sufficient amounts to purchase whatever they had been saving for. Second, they did not ring-fence any money to be saved but simply put aside whatever was left after they had met their other expenses. Consequently, savings tended to be the first thing cut back when they experienced other demands on their budget.

Circumstantial savers all worked to a clear save/spend cycle. At a micro level this meant that money saved for, say, a car or holiday was spent as soon as the required amount of money was saved. Across a lifetime, however, it meant that the periods during which saving money took on a high priority were punctuated with periods of spending during which no money was saved. Sometimes the focus of spending was purely for enjoyment. More often, circumstantial savers' ability to put money aside was undermined by other pressing demands on their household budget. This was the second key factor which explains the attitudes of circumstantial savers.

The circumstantial savers in our sample provide a clear view of the way in which their approach to saving was governed by their circumstances. The vast majority said that they had 'lived for the day' when they were younger and 'youth' was certainly perceived as a phase during which saving money need not be a priority. A woman in her late 20s commented:

> *When I was younger, before, when I lived with my mum and dad, everything I got I spent. I didn't put anything away.*

However, most of the younger circumstantial savers who were concentrating on enjoying life rather than worrying about saving money, still demonstrated a recognition that they would need to develop what they saw as a more 'responsible' attitude to saving as their lives progressed.

One couple now in their 40s provide a classic example of the effects of the lifecycle on saving. They saved regularly when they first got engaged and married but changed their approach when they started a family:

> *When I left work to have my son and we had a fair chunk of money in the bank and I was only off work for four years until he started school and during that period of time we didn't save anything and that money [in the bank] tied us over and my husband carried on working and then of course when [my son] was four, I started to go back to work and that was when we started putting a little bit of money away.*

So circumstantial savers among people at this stage in the lifecycle varied between those who were starting to 'enjoy life' again after the pressures of child rearing and those who were trying to accrue some security for their old age.

The effects of this spend-save cycle across the lifetime of a circumstantial saver is clearly apparent among many of the retired people with this attitude to saving. They could look back over their lives and identify several, sometimes quite lengthy, periods during which they had not considered saving at all. A man in his late 50s described this cycle very clearly:

> *I think there's a stage in your life where your expenditure takes up everything, you just can't save, you know. We went through this patch when we first got married... then the family comes along, and you still save, but as they get older you find they take more and more of your money then... you're looking to survive more than anything else at that point. As soon as they [leave home] you start to save again, looking towards your future.*

However, a number of factors can be identified which disrupted the lifecycle effect for some of the people in the sample. Some of these factors had more serious implications for long-term financial security. For example, experience of poor health lengthened periods of financial constraint at the expense of saving for old age. One circumstantial saver in the sample found herself swapping child-related expenses for crippling health-related expenses at a time in her life when she had anticipated having some money to spare and, in particular, to save for retirement. She said:

> *Well, you think when the children are grown up and married..., 'Oh well, now we can start planning for our future'. Had I still been working we could have done... But with just one wage, when you think he doesn't earn a very good wage...*

Non-savers

Non-savers in this context refers to general approaches to money rather than to current behaviour. Thus there were many people who were not saving at the time of the interview, such as chiefly circumstantial savers who were going through a spend-phase and dedicated savers who, having reached retirement, were determined to enjoy the money they had put aside. However, a very small number of people had never saved money in the past and had no plans to do so in the future. These people had not simply rejected or abandoned the idea of saving in the short-term. They were people who saw no point in saving at any time and were happy to simply 'live for the day', muddling through difficult times and worrying about the future when it arrived.

The key to understanding why some people did not feel that saving was important at all relates to the importance of personal circumstances and lifestyle factors which reduce the appropriateness of saving and investing money. The non-savers in the sample were starkly different from each other in terms of their lifestyles and personal circumstances. Yet both were experiencing a particular set of circumstances which meant that saving money was very difficult. This was the main force which shaped their attitude to saving.

In many respects, a rejection of the importance of saving might be seen as frivolous and ill-thought out. In fact, this approach to saving was formed in reaction to a range of factors, some relating back to childhood, which made living for the day seem a far more rational option than deferring gratification. For example, one man in his 30s was unusual because, although he and his partner had young children, he was determined to simply 'live for the day'. His attitude to saving had developed as a reaction *against* his parents' experience. His mother had taken a very strict attitude to saving, but his father had died before he could enjoy the benefits of the money they had accrued. Consequently, he had developed a strong feeling that it was far better to enjoy life because '*you cannot tell what the future holds*'. He earned quite a small and sometimes variable wage which meant that the amount of money that the family could reliably commit to regular saving did not seem worthwhile. In addition, his job was temporary and could end at any time. Consequently, planning ahead was not easy and this, too, encouraged a 'live for the day approach'. Perhaps most importantly, however, his job was physically demanding and often unpleasant. He felt very strongly that the only thing which made his working life bearable was knowing that he could use his wages for 'frivolities'.

The second non-saver interviewed, a single man in his 50s had equally little incentive to take a strict attitude to saving, although for slightly different reasons. Unlike the couple above, this man did not feel that he benefited more from spending, he believed that he had little to save for. His experience of growing up in a very poor family had resulted in a complete rejection of the notion of saving for a rainy day. He explained:

> *Well I never had nought as a kid... You see, I'm the youngest one of ten, and... all my clothes were hand-me-downs. So when I started work, I went out, and even today, I won't have nothing second hand... and I don't go out and buy one pair of shoes, I'll go and buy three, and I'll go and buy four shirts.*

More importantly, however, because he was single he was not concerned about accruing financial stability for his family or with having money to leave in bequests when he died. He remarked, *No well, I'm single... I don't care about what I leave behind, it don't bother me.* Because he felt that his behaviour did not impact on anyone but himself, he also saw little point in saving for old age:

> *I don't see the sense in me thinking, 'Oh well, I've got to save this for my old age'... the old people who say, 'I've got to save enough to bury me'. Why bother? Someone's going to bury you... Why save £2,000 and sit freezing... I've seen [elderly people] they're frightened to put the gas fire on because they've got to spend their savings because their son that lives in Spain or somewhere has got to bury them. And I think, 'Well, stuff it! Enjoy your flaming money'.*

Consequently, given that he had nobody to support and nobody to leave money to when he died, he felt it was important to spend it on himself and to enjoy a good standard of living while he was alive.

In general, therefore, people tended to have positive attitudes towards saving – where attitudes were more negative, this was usually due to circumstances. For example, one person said that although it was important to save in theory, this was very difficult in practice:

> *Yes, at the moment, we live for the day. We haven't got any money spare – you have to live for the day.*

ATTITUDES TO HOUSING WEALTH

Having looked at general attitudes towards saving, we now turn to attitudes towards accumulating housing wealth. Numerous advantages to home ownership were mentioned. Buying a home was seen as a good way of saving money rather than paying money to a landlord. Rent was seen as 'dead money' and was generally considered to be expensive compared with a mortgage. It was therefore seen as a good investment for one's own future and one's children and the recent experience of negative equity had not shaken everyone's faith in the security of investing in housing.

Another advantage was that buying a home gave more choice about where to live and the type of property lived in. This was particularly important to people who were thinking of starting a family. People were buying the ability to live in particular neighbourhoods which were perceived to be safe and suitable places to raise a family (for example, they were close to 'good' schools). There was also a feeling that buying a home in particular areas was more of a guarantee of good neighbours and, if the neighbours became a problem, home owners were more able to move than council tenants.

Although respondents were generally very favourable about owning a home, there were also some drawbacks mentioned. For example, although buying a home might give choice about where to live, it also tied you to a particular place and if you had made a poor choice of area or neighbours, you were dependent on the housing market to move (and moving was costly). So renting was seen as providing more flexibility and this was valued mostly by younger people. Older people were more concerned about the costs of maintaining and repairing their own home when their incomes were lower than they had been, and when they were widowed and so could not rely on their husbands to deal with such matters. Some young people had also bought homes which needed considerable attention. They had seen this as a long-term investment but in the short run it meant that most of their spare money was diverted towards their home.

Paying into a mortgage was also associated with a number of concerns which were shared by those who currently had mortgages as well as those without. The main concern was about signing a commitment to pay a mortgage over such a long period given uncertainties about job security. Linked to this, there was a general awareness that the government had cut back on providing help to unemployed people with mortgages and this added to existing anxieties:

> *I'm not sure of my facts but I don't even think they help with mortgages anymore.*

There was also concern about the uncertainty surrounding interest rates. Many respondents had had mortgages during the late 1980s when mortgage interest rates had increased dramatically, and although most had managed to maintain their payments, this experience had nevertheless shaken their faith in future economic stability. The interviews took place when interest rates had been rising slightly in response to increases in consumer spending:

The shadow of negative equity still hung over many people, even those who had not experienced it in the past. All in all, a mortgage was seen as a debt rather than a way of saving. One woman admitted that: '*I wish it was paid off, it's always a worry*'. For some people, the mortgage had always been a struggle to pay. One woman, who had paid off 21 years of her 25-year mortgage, still felt concern about it and said that she would only relax once it had all been paid off :

> *In the early stages of the mortgage it is a millstone because it's usually quite a large percentage of your income and as you get a bit older it becomes a smaller percentage but there is always the doubt that if you, yourself, or your husband become ill and we couldn't afford to pay the mortgage ... we might still have problems and not fortunately end it.*

Some of the most negative comments about home-ownership and mortgages came from the three ex-mortgagors interviewed. One was a man who was now retired and had lost his house in his divorce settlement. Another was of working age but said that he would not buy a house again. He had lost his home after being made redundant and now saw the advantages of renting from the council because full rent would be paid during times of unemployment. He therefore felt that renting gave greater security than home-owning:

> *It's being mercenary now but if I fall out of work, which is more likely now than it is ever, then I go to the council and the council pay my rent, so I'm not bothered, I don't lose my house. If I've got a mortgage and I fall out of work I could lose my house because all they pay is the interest, maybe. So if I rent a property, I'm guaranteed to keep it.*

So home ownership was associated with security but mortgages were associated with insecurity and risk. People were very keen to finish paying their mortgage and one couple said that they paid off their mortgage early (when they retired), despite financial advice to the contrary because they wanted to have it out of the way.

ATTITUDES TO PENSION WEALTH

Although mortgages caused anxiety, they were seen as more important than paying into a private pension. Mortgages provided a current benefit – one's home – which was consumable at the same time as saving towards buying it. Any benefit from a private pension could only be consumed in the future and the future had too many uncertainties about it.

Most respondents agreed that it was becoming increasingly important to have a private (that is, either an occupational or personal) pension. This was not just because they had concerns about the *level* of the state pension when they retired but also because they had considerable doubts about whether it would exist at all:

> *I don't know what Labour's going to do about that ... we've got to wait and see. I mean, are they going to change everything? You know, we're just up in the air now, we don't know what's going to happen.*

There was widespread awareness about the current level of the state pension among non-pensioners – mainly because many of their own parents were receiving it. It was felt that the level was very low and most respondents recognised that this would not be enough to meet their aspirations for retirement. Most wished to maintain their current standard of living, which they thought would be much easier once their mortgage was paid off and other outgoings – such as spending on children – would be much lower. Some were considering moving to smaller housing, but did not necessarily see this as 'trading down' as they wanted to move up in quality even if they moved down in terms of size. So if they were not planning to release equity from their homes to finance a decent lifestyle in retirement, pension arrangements were very important to secure the kind of lifestyle which most aspired to.

Although most people saw advantages to private pension provision, some thought that it was a risky investment because they might die before they could benefit from it. This view was particularly common among working class people, who do indeed have lower life expectancies than middle class people. Linked to this view about life expectancy is a desire to avoid thinking about old age. One retired person himself admitted that it had always been difficult to imagine getting older:

> *When you're younger, you don't, you can't think of yourself getting old.*

More details from the qualitative study about how people accumulated housing and pension wealth are given in the next chapter.

ATTITUDES TO RUNNING DOWN WEALTH

Much more attention has been paid to the accumulation of wealth than dis-saving (the running down of wealth) even though the main reason to accumulate wealth is to be able to use it up at some point. For example, young people may save up for a deposit on a flat or house but the bulk of dis-saving is likely to occur when people are older or retired. The people interviewed for this study expressed very clear and generally well-considered ideas about running down savings and assets. Many also had some experience of doing so. Attitudes to *running down* savings and assets:

- differed depending on different types of wealth
- were surprisingly consistent between people of different social classes, lifecycle groups and with different levels of knowledge about savings and assets
- related most strongly to general approaches to wealth accumulation.

In short, people's attitudes and experiences of running down savings and assets represented a hierarchy which was driven by their overall attitude to saving. Dedicated savers were reluctant to use up any of their savings and assets in the short-term and often planned to continue saving after retirement. They were only prepared to consider running down their savings and assets in emergencies or if faced with a situation when their only alternative was to borrow. They were extremely resistant to borrowing, preferring to go without, and the only circumstance in which borrowing was perceived to be preferable to drawing on their savings was if the latter meant they would incur financial penalties.

Despite their resistance to spending in the short-term, dedicated savers were especially keen to enjoy the wealth they had accrued when they reached old age and, sometimes, were prepared to spend money rather than pass it on to their children. They did, however, tend to plan to leave their properties in bequests.

Circumstantial savers' attitudes to saving were heavily influenced by actual ability to save. Their feelings about running down savings and assets was similarly pragmatic. Although they were cautious about cashing in pensions or insurance and endowment policies, they were more prepared to think about releasing some of their housing or mortgage wealth and they had no qualms at all about spending financial savings. Consequently, they had more liberal attitudes to borrowing and were prepared to take on bank loans or even use a credit card if they had no savings to draw on. Circumstantial savers planned to use their savings in the short-term for both necessities and luxuries. However, most were concerned to keep something aside for emergencies and hoped to have sufficient money to enjoy their old age and leave something in bequests for their children or families.

Non-savers were in a very different position because their situations and attitudes to saving meant that they had little in the form of savings or assets to run down. Their rejection of saving in favour of spending meant that any money they had did not last long. Consequently, they were often faced with financial insecurity which forced them to draw on any money they did have. Non-savers were prepared to run down any form of savings or assets which were available and they did not plan for the future at all.

Reasons not to dis-save

Some people who had accumulated wealth did not wish to use it up. One of the main reasons for this was because they wished to make a bequest. There are a number of reasons why people may wish to leave bequests: they may want to help their children or friends or favourite causes in a spirit of altruism; they may want to influence others after they have died by making a bequest which is conditional on particular behaviour (such as remaining in the family business); other people may leave money because of uncertainty about how long they will live.

From our interviews it seems that the biggest influence on attitudes to running down assets, was the desire to leave something to their children or families when they died. This was a key preoccupation, even among quite young respondents, and was clearly an important determinant of their wish to accrue some financial stability over a lifetime. Plans to safeguard some savings and/or assets to leave in bequests were apparent among the vast majority of dedicated and circumstantial savers, but there were some differences between and within these two groups. Generally, housing wealth was ring-fenced for bequests and financial wealth was considered available for spending in old age. A woman in her late 50s who was expecting to retire shortly explained:

> *I'd like to leave my house to my children, but my money I'd like to spend. Because I feel that I never had anything from our parents, they didn't buy their houses, so our own children, today, if their parents have got houses are going to be very lucky... But my own money, I'd like to spend it and enjoy it.*

In reality, however, most expected to leave some of their financial savings as well because they were uncertain about how long they would live and wanted to ensure that they could support themselves even if they became very old.

The changing nature of lifecycle patterns caused complications in some cases as divorce and re-partnering made lines of bequest less clear. A man in his 40s had had to plan a very complex arrangement, to ensure that he could pass on some of his savings and assets to the children of his first marriage without offending his second wife and step-daughter.

Using up financial savings

Savings are the most liquid form of wealth and so would be the easiest to deplete should one wish to do so. Once again, we know little about which people run down their savings, why they do this, and at what stages of their life they are at.

When dedicated savers reached retirement, however, most found that spending their financial savings was more difficult than they had anticipated. Saving had become a hard habit to break and with few things that they wanted to do or buy, they found themselves continuing to keep financial savings aside in order to pass them on to their children and grandchildren.

The majority of circumstantial savers could not conceive of the idea of saving money without planning to spend it. This is closely linked with their overall attitude to saving, which focused on saving for particular or short-term goals, resulting in save-spend cycles, or as one circumstantial saver described it 'save and splurge'. So, one single man in his mid-20s remarked:

> *Obviously you've got to spend. It'd be insane if you didn't. If the money was there, say, and you wanted a car and it would make your life easier then, yes, I wouldn't have a problem about spending money.*

Another, older circumstantial saver, a single man in his late 60s spent his savings on travel, his view was, 'Why not live? You're a long time dead, is what I keep being told'.

However, circumstantial savers were not cavalier or irresponsible in their attitude to running down financial savings. Most had plans to keep money aside as a 'float' for emergencies or to cover old age. Some ring-fenced part of their savings for this purpose, others kept an amount of money in mind that they wanted to have when they retired. One said:

> *Be cautious of what you're doing. Because it's alright spending all your money on holidays, and then you find out you're going to live a bit longer than what you thought. I'd sooner find at the end of the day, that there's money left after I've gone, rather than the pot is empty [and think], 'What do I do now?'. So I say you've got to be sensible about these things... you don't spend unless you've got it.*

Unlocking housing wealth

Wiener (1994) argues that (p94) 'the elderly live too poor and die too rich'. He argues that this is not largely because of the desire to bequeath but because of the difficulties involved in running down assets, particularly housing assets. Most of the marketable wealth held by the majority of retired people is in the form of housing wealth.

Equity release schemes are most advanced in the US, but research in the UK suggests that there is limited demand for equity release instruments because reverse mortgages increase incomes by very small amounts and are of no use to people with very little housing wealth. Mackintosh *et al* (1990) estimated that 80 per cent of owner-occupied households headed by someone aged 65–74 had housing equity of about £40,000 in 1989. As we shall see in the next chapter, analysis of the *Family Resources Survey* showed that in 1995/6, half of all pensioner couples and a quarter of all single pensioners had housing equity of at least £57,000 and half of all single pensioners had housing equity of at least £30,000. It has been estimated that releasing equity of £30,000 will only provide about £200 a month in retirement income, so the amount of money which might be unlocked is unlikely to sustain people unless it is used to supplement another source of income.

In the qualitative research, attitudes and experiences of running down housing or mortgage wealth were, again, largely driven by general approaches to saving money, but some other influences were also apparent.

Dedicated savers were generally not in favour of running down housing or mortgage wealth under any circumstances for two reasons. First, because they were unhappy about using up the money which was tied up in their home, preferring to use other sources of finance (so that they could leave their housing wealth to their children). Second, because owning their own home was a key element of the security that dedicated savers were trying to attain and they were very uncomfortable at the idea of giving up that security.

While circumstantial savers had the same emotional attachment to their homes, and did not want to think about selling them, particularly for purely financial motives, they were, again, realistic about the circumstances which would warrant a revision of this position. Consequently, they had more liberal opinions regarding most methods of running down housing or mortgage wealth. For circumstantial savers in social class AB this was, at least partly, related to issues around status. They did not feel that being a tenant afforded the same status as home ownership.

Circumstantial savers from social classes C, D or E, however, were not as strongly opposed to the idea of moving into rented property. This was particularly the case for those who had lived in rented housing when they were younger.

These liberal attitudes did not extend to equity release schemes and circumstantial savers expressed views very similar to dedicated savers on this issue. They expressed far greater unease at the idea of a third party owning part of their equity while they remained in the house than they did over second mortgages, tending to feel that equity release schemes would somehow be intrusive to their lives.

Pensions, insurance policies and other assets

Amongst most of those interviewed, pensions, insurance policies and other similar assets were not regarded as money which was easily available and which could be used as and when necessary. This was primarily because all of these forms of saving were viewed as long-term commitments which carried negative consequences if they were not sustained. Circumstantial savers expressed similarly cautious attitudes to using up this type of wealth but were not in as strong a position as the dedicated savers always to avoid doing so. None of the circumstantial savers in the study thought that cashing in an endowment policy early was a good idea. They clearly recognised that while running down money might solve some short-term problems, it would merely 'store up' trouble in the longer term. This feeling became stronger among circumstantial savers as they approached retirement age. One woman explained that she and her husband would never consider using the money that he had put aside in an endowment policy because '*well, my husband's counting down to retirement day*'.

However, there was a view that, if money was desperately needed, then endowment policies might have to be cashed in early. A lone mother had cashed in an insurance policy early after her marriage broke down and, unable to manage the mortgage alone, was in danger of having her home repossessed. In fact, she got very little money from the policy and did, indeed, lose her home but, given that the insurance policy was the only 'spare' money she had available, she had little choice but to use it.

Non-savers, on the other hand, did not display any of these concerns and their experiences of running down savings and assets demonstrate this clearly. One, a man in his 30s with a young family, having cashed in his life insurance policy at the age of 32, had no form of savings or investment at all at the time of the interviews. Another, a single man in his late 50s who had taken early retirement on health grounds, had paid into a pension throughout his working life. He had, however, already used up all of the lump sum he had received from his pension when he retired. He had spent part of the money on travel, which gave him pleasure and was something he had always promised himself he would do when he retired:

> *I spent about three and a half [thousand] going to Australia and Dubai and Singapore and Bangkok and Thailand and... Well, I thought if I don't do it when I had the money, straight away... So I thought 'Right, I'll go and see them'.*

He had been forced to use the remainder, however, to pay for essential repairs to his house because he had no other savings to draw on. He explained;

> *I kept saying 'Oh, I want four hundred pound to pay this. I want a hundred and fifty to pay that. I want six hundred out'. So over the years the money got less, the interest got less, and now I've got an empty account!*

INCENTIVES AND DISINCENTIVES TO SAVE

Attitudes and behaviour with regard to savings and wealth may be affected by various social and economic policies. These policies may create, in theory, incentives and disincentives to save. However, whether these policies affect behaviour depends, in practice, first of all on whether people know about their existence and then on attitudes towards them. The findings from the qualitative research give some insight into the possible incentive or disincentive effects of the tax and social security systems.

The impact of the taxation system

When asked whether they knew that the tax system offered some benefits to particular types of saving or investment, about half of the people interviewed said that they knew virtually nothing about this:

> *I don't know anything about it! I mean I know there are differ-ent types but I don't know what they are and what they're for to be honest. I don't really tend to pay too much attention to them.*

Among the other half of the sample, most had a vague awareness that the taxation system treated particular types of assets, like National Savings, in different ways but respondents had little idea about the details. A few respondents had a reasonably good grasp of the way the tax system worked in relation to assets. Differences in knowledge were mostly related to social class and amount of money invested. Those from higher social classes and with large amounts to invest generally knew more about the tax system.

A significant minority of respondents were aware of mortgage interest relief (and they were also aware that this was being cut back). They were mostly also aware that private pensions attracted tax relief and lower National Insurance contributions. Some also mentioned that the interest on their shares was tax free. Most people had a general idea that TESSAs provided tax free interest but not everyone understood this – one person thought TESSAs were only for non-tax payers. There was a general belief that non-tax payers could get special deals with their savings, but not everyone knew quite how and where these deals could be found.

Even where respondents were aware of various tax differ-ences, it was believed that the advantages were too small to influence their behaviour in a significant way. No one would take out a mortgage just because of MIRAS (even though they were not happy about it being cut back). Pensions were seen as relatively more attractive because of their tax status, but this had not and did not particularly encourage people to take out a pension. Other more fundamental factors had more of an effect on both mortgages and private pensions. These were: ability to afford a mortgage and a private pension; general attitudes to mortgages and private pensions; easy access to a mortgage and pension scheme which was considered safe. People did, however, admit that tax advantages had encouraged them to take out TESSAs and National Savings for children. But they did not claim that these schemes encouraged them to save *more* money, they merely encouraged them to save it in different ways. Nevertheless, TESSAs and National Savings were not very widespread forms of saving in the sample, mainly because people had little money to save and preferred to put the little they had into what they saw as, more accessible bank or building society accounts.

Asset rules around social security and long-term care

Respondents were asked about their knowledge of how the social security system treated assets. Most people had an idea, or at least guessed, that some social security benefits were unavailable to people with a certain level of savings. But because of the way they were selected (we deliberately excluded very poor families – see Appendix C), most had never claimed means-tested benefits and so had not personally come across the savings rule. Nor did these people think that they would ever need to claim these benefits in the future. For the most part, these people were either in relatively secure jobs or they believed that if they were to lose their jobs they would find other work fairly quickly. And if they were only temporarily unemployed, these people would probably receive a contributory-based benefit and so would not be subjected to a means test.

Those who had received means-tested benefits in the past thought that they might need to do so at some point in the future due to the insecurities of their employment. But they had such difficulties in saving due to low income that their awareness of the capital rules was not a factor in their savings behaviour. One woman, however, said that if she had saved money and then needed to claim a means-tested benefit, she would lie about her savings in order to claim. Like many others, she thought that it was very unfair for the system to penalise her thrift. This echoes the views of respondents from another study who saw non-declaration of savings as a less serious form of benefit fraud than other types such as non-declaration of earnings (Rowlingson *et al,*

1997). Criticism of the system came particularly from working class people who had generally worked and saved but who had also sometimes needed assistance from the benefit system. A respondent in her 50s took a similar view:

> *I have seen people through my life who – two people earning the same amount of money through their life and one taking the 'saving for a rainy day' attitude and the other one spending. The one that has taken the attitude of 'spend today, live tomorrow' has come out better when he has got to his old age because he has been able to claim everything that is going and the other one has got his little bit of savings ... It seems very unfair..*

Another respondent felt that 'middle England' was particularly penalised by the rules:

> *People who save all their life ... are penalised because they are thrifty, yet anybody who has spent every penny they have got ... they get all the help in the world ... the best thing is you've either got to have loads of money or not – in between you are just missing out all the time.*

The social security system not only takes into account the amount of assets that people have, but also their income. One man said that he had actually been penalised, as he saw it, when he retired early and received a pension which then affected his entitlement to means-tested benefits.

If there was disgruntlement about the rules on means-tested social security benefits, there was outright condemnation of the rules on long-term care. Respondents had a vague awareness that assets were taken into account if someone went into long-term care. Some people – usually those who had found out about the rules on behalf of an elderly relative – even had a good idea of the thresholds. Most people seemed more aware, and more concerned, about the possibility of having to sell one's home to pay for care than having to pay for care from financial savings. Whatever their level of knowledge about the rules, all respondents thought that long-term care should be free for everyone regardless of means, and many thought that the current level of income tax and national insurance should be enough to cover it.

> *[My partner] has a vast amount of tax taken off his wages every week, plus national insurance and I can say the only time I've ever been in hospital is when I've had the two kids. I haven't cost the Health Service anything ... where's the money going?*

Another respondent expressed a very general view:

> *I don't think we should have to sell our properties to keep us in residential care, not at all, because I think when people have worked all their lives, what are they getting out of their money that they've paid into? ... In other words, you might just as well not have bought your home in the first place.*

Others thought that direct taxes should be increased to meet the costs if necessary. One woman did have some sympathy with the rules, pointing out that increasing life expectancy made long-term care very expensive. Others recognised that the extended family was less likely to help with care these days compared with the past.

Although most people knew about the rules on long-term care and disagreed violently with them, their savings and home-buying behaviour did not seem to be affected. For many, particularly the young, the prospect of needing long-term care was too far away to seem a real prospect – it was even further away than retirement, which seemed far enough. Most thought it unlikely that they would need such care – they thought that they would die before they were too ill or infirm to look after themselves, or that their relatives would care for them. Some were adamant that they would never go into long-term care because they hated the very idea, with loss of independence being the main concern. One woman said that '*I'd rather they shot me [than go into long-term care]*'. For many, particularly older people, the very prospect of needing long-term care was such an awful one that they pushed it out of their minds – the financial aspect of long-term care was not the main issue. In some cases, the rules about long-term care were used as an additional minor reason, or in some ways perhaps, an excuse, for not saving more money. The rules did not constitute a major real disincentive to save or buy a home.

Only one person said that she would like to save or insure towards the cost of long-term care, but did not think that she could really afford to do so. People generally felt that if they did find themselves in a position of needing care, they would sell their homes in advance or trade down and give their money to their children rather than give the money to the Treasury. This was the nub of the discontent over the rules – people believed passionately that they should have a right to pass on their housing wealth to their children.

$$4$$
—

Accumulating Different Types of Wealth

In Chapters 2 and 3, we looked at the overall links between income, wealth and the lifecycle as well as knowledge of, and attitudes towards wealth. In this chapter, we focus on the accumulation of particular types of wealth, namely financial savings, housing wealth and pension wealth.

FINANCIAL ASSETS

Financial assets are among the most liquid form of assets, although money is sometimes tied up for particular periods of time in saving or investment schemes with higher rates of return. In Britain, the two most commonly held financial asset groups are IBAs (interest-bearing accounts such as bank/building society accounts and savings clubs) and National Savings (Banks *et al*, 1994). Then there are Tax Exempt Special Savings Accounts (TESSAs) and Personal Equity Plans (PEPs). Remaining wealth splits into equities and 'other'.

A picture of financial assets

The *Family Resources Survey* shows that wealth in the form of financial assets represented a minority of overall wealth. Only 17 per cent of total wealth (including state and private pensions) was in the form of these most liquid of assets and, in fact, just over one third of families had no financial assets at all. Young single

Table 4.1 Financial wealth grouped around the non-zero median by lifecycle group

Column percentages	Young singles	Older singles	Young childless couples	Lone parents	Young couples, young children	Older couples, young children	Couples, school-age children	Older childless couples	Pensioner couples	Single pensioners	All
Financial wealth:											
0	52	43	23	74	38	29	31	22	19	34	37
>0 but <3,705	36	28	48	22	40	33	36	29	23	30	32
£3,705 or more	13	30	29	5	22	38	33	49	58	36	32

Source: 1995/6 *Family Resources Survey*

Table 4.2 Percentage of lifecycle groups with one or more of these accounts

					Lifecycle group						
	Young singles	Older singles	Young childless couples	Lone parents	Young couples, young children	Older couples, young children	Older Couples, school-age children	Older childless couples	Pensioner couples	Single pensioners	All
% with:											
Current	75	70	94	54	88	92	90	89	79	58	77
Post Office	8	7	10	9	15	22	23	8	13	11	11
TESSA	3	12	7	2	6	10	11	21	16	8	10
Other building society	36	44	67	32	61	67	67	62	60	45	51
Other bank	13	14	26	14	20	24	27	21	18	17	18
Other account	1	2	3	1	2	2	2	4	3	2	2
Gilts	0	1	0	0	0	1	1	2	3	2	1
Unit trusts	2	6	5	1	4	6	6	10	9	3	5
Stocks/shares	7	17	19	4	17	28	23	31	27	14	18
National Savings	1	4	2	4	10	16	9	6	17	9	7
SAYE	1	2	5	0	3	3	3	4	1	0	2
Premium Bonds	12	22	24	11	25	40	36	36	36	20	25
PEPs	2	7	7	1	5	8	8	14	10	4	7
N	5,420	3,837	1,335	2,033	2,327	872	3,309	4,753	3,029	4,570	31,485
Row per cent	17	12	4	7	7	3	11	15	10	15	100

Source: 1995/6 *Family Resources Survey*

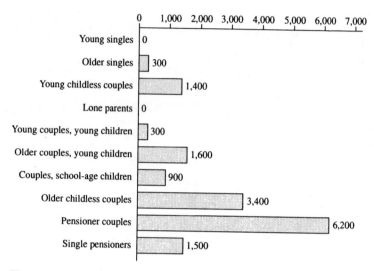

Figure 4.1 Median financial wealth by lifecycle groups (£)

people and lone parents had the lowest holdings of such wealth. Three-quarters of lone parents and a half of young single people had no money saved at all (Table 4.1). At the other extreme, almost 60 per cent of pensioner couples and almost a half of older childless couples had financial assets with a value greater than or equal to the non-zero median of £3,700. Only 5 per cent of lone parents had financial assets as substantial as £3,700.

Figure 4.1 shows median financial wealth by lifecycle group – pensioner couples have most (approximately £6,000), followed by older childless couples (approximately £3,000).

There are, however, a number of ways of storing financial assets. Methods of saving differ in their associated benefits, such as interest rates and degrees of liquidity. Although we have been unable to see what proportions of the wealth for each lifecycle type are located in certain types of financial account (as figures for financial wealth were derived for some families – see Chapter 1 for further details), it has been possible to examine the popularity of different accounts for the families in the sample. All families were asked about any accounts they held. Table 4.2 shows that current accounts were the most popular of financial accounts. Seventy-seven per cent of families had at least one current account.

In line with previous research on money management, Kempson (1994) found that people in very disadvantaged financial situations were less likely to use bank accounts at all. They felt more secure managing their finances on a cash basis. Analysis of the FRS shows that interest-bearing accounts such as current accounts and building society accounts were less common for groups at the lower end of the income distribution – younger groups and older groups. The lifecycle groups with the very lowest income levels also stood out in having low levels of such accounts. Only 54 per cent of lone parents had current accounts. Previous research also suggests, however, that those on low incomes who do have financial assets are more likely to have them in interest bearing accounts than in stocks and shares or other more profitable schemes (McKay, 1992). Single pensioners were also less likely to have current accounts, and they were substantially less likely to have current accounts than were the pensioner couples (58 per cent compared with 79 per cent).

After the interest-bearing current and building society accounts, the next most popular way of saving financial assets was in the form of premium bonds. A quarter of all families had some premium bonds, the proportion rising for older couples with pre-school age children (to 40 per cent), young couples with school age children (36 per cent), older childless couples (36 per cent) and older, retired couples (36 per cent).

About one in five (18 per cent) of all families had money in stocks and shares. Young single people and lone parents were least likely to have money in such schemes. The proportions of families who owned shares were higher for high income groups. Almost a third of older childless couples had some wealth in stocks and shares, as did 28 per cent of older couples with pre-school age children. Pensioner couples, although characterised by low income levels, were asset rich and were almost as likely to have stocks and shares as the previous two high income groups. These and the older childless couples were more likely to own PEPs, too.

About one family in ten had a TESSA – older childless couples and pensioner couples were most likely to have wealth in this form (21 per cent and 16 per cent respectively). Only 7 per cent of families had PEPs – once again these were most common among older childless couples (14 per cent) and pensioner couples (10 per cent). Young single people and lone parents were least likely of all groups to have TESSAs or PEPs.

Saving money in different ways

The qualitative research investigated how and why people came to have different types of financial assets. One non-working woman's comments sum up the general views about different types of financial saving:

> *National Savings – I don't know much about them, just that they've been going a long time. Premium Bonds – they seem like old things ... and they seem perhaps a bit old fashioned. I think the National Savings have a very good interest rate. Premium Bonds are a bit risky – you might not come up – whereas I'd rather know I was getting something. TESSAs – they've been advertised a lot and I like the idea of them. PEPs – I don't know enough about PEPs – I know a little bit about them but not all that much. Stocks, shares, bonds, unit trusts... I wouldn't really consider them suitable for someone like me.*

Importance of the lifecycle and social class

Lifecycle stage was an important factor in relation to financial assets. For example, most people, particularly in the younger groups, recalled that they had opened a savings account when they had been children. People also began saving at other key lifecycle stages such as leaving home and getting married. For families with children, much of their saving was directed specifically towards their children. They were putting money aside for their children's future rather than for their own. Among the pre-retired group, many were trying to save for their retirement, but most were finding it very difficult to do so, given their low incomes. Among the retired people, some had considerable financial assets but, in some cases, were still trying to add to these. This was partly because they had got into the habit of saving but also because many were still in their 60s and so expected to live quite a lot longer and did not want to use up their savings too soon

Social class was also an important factor. Working class people, and those on low incomes, were much more keen on banks, building societies, National Savings, premium bonds and insurance policies. Middle class people were more likely to have stocks and shares, TESSAs and PEPs. This was mainly related to the fact that working class people had relatively little to save and so tended to want methods which were safe and trustworthy. For example, insurance policies seemed to be particularly popular among those with relatively low incomes and assets as they were seen as a secure way of investing for children without the possibility that they would be dipped into if money became short. Policies were set up so that they would mature when their child turned a particular age and then the money would be given directly to the child for spending on whatever they wished. Other people took out insurance policies for themselves. One woman talked about how she had been brought up with the old 'penny policies' that her parents and grandparents had taken out:

> *Endowment policies – on your life and that – it's sort of handed down to you. Your parents did it and it's something you automatically do ... They had the old penny policies, you were brought up with it, so it was an automatic thing ... you took them out when you got married or when you were old enough and you were working.*

Confidence and trust in finance companies

A number of themes arose during the qualitative interviews. For example, as mentioned in Chapter 3, confidence and trust in a company and a scheme are vitally important in financial dealings, and these themes will occur again when mortgages and pensions are discussed. Most people went to the companies that parents or friends recommended. One woman, however, was unusual in shopping around when she wanted to invest in a PEP. She eventually chose to save with Virgin Direct, mainly because she felt that this was a company she could trust. Their advertising, public relations and the persona of the head of the company had created a very positive and confidence-inspiring corporate image as far as she was concerned:

> *The actual company and everything it stands for instils confidence ... [It was] a name that I knew and that I felt I could trust. I mean I might be quite naive about that but I don't know ... I'd also read good things about them.*

Corporate image is therefore important and, it seems, is becoming increasingly important in the financial services sector. Groups of companies which generally have a good corporate image are the well-known supermarket chains such as Tesco, Sainsbury and

Marks & Spencer. It will therefore be interesting to gauge the success with which they have moved into the personal finance field.

Active and passive saving

Another interesting theme is that very often people start saving – and saving in particular ways – more through 'accident' than positive action. Rather than actively deciding that they want to save for a particular reason and then finding the best way to do so, people are presented with a way of saving which they then take up, only considering afterwards what they might use the money for. This reversal of the commonly assumed saving process also occurs in some circumstances with borrowing. For example, people sometimes borrow money without a clear purpose and only decide what to do with it afterwards (Rowlingson, 1995).

This kind of accidental or 'passive' saving can be seen in relation to insurance policies which many people had found out about because their parents used them. They often took them out with the same companies that their parents had used. One woman said that she had been too 'lazy' to shop around for the best deal. But laziness is probably only a small part of the story – she could feel confident in the company and the scheme, having seen her parents use them successfully in the past. And she had little time to spend searching for the best scheme.

Passive saving can also be seen in relation to shares. One woman explained:

> I mean I've had [British Gas shares] a long time ... and I've never bothered since. I mean I've still got them and that's it ... I recently had a circular asking if I wanted to keep them or sell them but I decided that I would actually just keep them, I don't know why ... really it's money that I'd forgotten about.

Some people accumulated shares passively when building societies converted to banks. Others had inherited shares from relatives who had died.

Methods of paying into savings/investments

In terms of paying money into different savings or investment schemes, people also preferred methods which required little positive action. Schemes such as the Save as You Earn and Share Save, which took money directly out of wages or directly out of a current account (through a standing order), were seen as the best way to save. This meant that the money was not missed. As one man said:

> *It's straight out of your wages, you don't see it. It's not a case of having to think, 'Oh. I could put it away or I might spend it on this', so it goes straight out of the wage.*

For those on lower incomes, personal collection from the door was seen as an added bonus with endowment policies:

> *We phoned up Royal Insurance and they said they'd collect it from the door and they'd send somebody out. And we thought it was a great idea because if somebody was on our doorstep asking for the money, we've got to give it to them!*

They felt that if money was *collected* by the company rather than actively *paid by the saver*, they were less likely to spend it on other things.

Inheritance

'Passive' saving is a term which can also be applied to inheriting money. The Royal Commission on the Distribution of Income and Wealth estimated that, in 1973, total inheritances bore a ratio of about 20 per cent to total wealth, so inheritance is a major means of accumulating wealth. Within a married couple, assets usually transfer to the widow or widower, with only a relatively small amount finding its way to other family members. When a single person dies, most wealth passes to the next generation and, on average, the wealth is divided among 2.3 people (Munroe, 1988). Given current life expectancy, these inheriting 'children' are likely to be in their 50s and 60s and many will have significant assets themselves (especially in the form of owner-occupation). Thus inheritance does not particularly help those struggling to accumulate assets but merely adds to the wealth of those already with assets.

In the qualitative research, people were asked about whether they expected to inherit any money in the future. Few said that they expected anything, at least in the short or medium term, and this reflects previous research by Ormerod and Willmott (1989), which found that only 14 per cent of people expected to inherit. Most respondents said that they hoped that their parents would live well into old age and any money (mainly that tied up in housing equity) would then be distributed among themselves and other siblings. As we have already seen, people find it difficult to contemplate their own future retirement, they also feel uneasy about contemplating the future death of their parents.

Changing patterns of family life also caused complications and uncertainties about inheritance. For example, one man's father had re-married and so there was doubt as to who he would leave his money to. Most people viewed the prospect of inheritance as a possibility rather than something that they could plan around. Some said that they would spend any inheritance straight away. Others said that they would pass it straight on to their children. Due to the uncertainties about inheritance – in terms of timing and possible amount – current financial behaviour was not affected by any prospects of inheritance and respondents said that they would view any actual inheritance as a bonus when it happened, rather than as something they could plan their future finances around.

Given the increase in owner-occupation and the increasing importance of housing wealth, inherited wealth is likely to play an even more widespread role in asset-accumulation, furthering the divide between the 'haves' and the 'have-nots'.

HOUSING WEALTH

As just mentioned, housing has become an increasingly important source of wealth in Britain in the last 20 years but, although it is a marketable form of wealth, the housing market is highly variable and wealth can only be realised through trading down, moving to rented accommodation or taking advantage of an equity release scheme.

In the early 20th century, housing was not considered to be a favourable form of investment. Even some relatively wealthy people preferred to remain tenants rather than tie up their capital in home ownership (Kemp, 1982). In 1918 only 10 per cent of dwellings in Britain were owner-occupied. In 1990, the figure was 66 per cent, according to the General Household Survey. Of course, owner-occupiers usually have mortgages and so do not own wealth to the full extent of the value of their property. According to the Royal Commission on the Distribution of Income and Wealth, housing represented 17 per cent of net personal wealth in 1960 in the UK. By 1975, this figure had reached 37 per cent and by 1985 (according to Hamnett *et al*, 1989), it was 48 per cent. As we saw in Chapter 2, analysis of the FRS shows that, if we exclude state pension (as is usually the case in these calculations), housing wealth accounted for 47 per cent of total wealth in 1995/6.

A picture of housing wealth

We now turn back to the *Family Resources Survey* to look at the distribution of housing wealth. Not all families have wealth in the form of housing assets. One third of families were renting their homes and so had no housing wealth. The proportion in rented accommodation was highest for younger and older age groups (Table 4.3). At least 40 per cent of families headed by someone aged 16 to 29, and by individuals aged 80 or more, were renting, compared with less than a quarter of those aged 40 to 59. Housing tenure was firmly related to lifecycle group, too. Fully 69 per cent of lone parents were renting, compared with only 13 per cent of older couples with pre-school age children and 16 per cent of older childless couples (Table 4.4).

Linked to differences in tenure, housing wealth differed markedly by lifecycle group (Table 4.5). Fully 89 per cent of young single people had no housing assets at all. Of young people who did have housing assets, the value of their housing wealth was below the non-zero median of about £52,000. This relates to the fact that most young people who do have mortgages will only be beginning to pay back their loans. Young childless couples were much more likely to be home-owners but again their level of housing wealth was fairly low. This analysis suggests that housing is related more closely to lifecycle effects than age – people take out a mortgage after a particular lifecycle trigger, such as finding a partner, rather than when they reach a particular age threshold.

Nevertheless, housing wealth was strongly related to the age of the family head. Older groups had high levels of housing wealth, no doubt indicating how advanced a stage people had

Table 4.3 Tenure type by age groups

| | | | | | Age groups | | | | |
	16–19	20–29	30–39	40–49	50–59	60–69	70–79	80+	All
Tenure:									
Owner/mortgage	57	54	68	76	75	69	62	56	66
Rent	41	44	31	23	24	29	37	41	33
Other	2	2	1	1	1	1	1	3	1

Source: 1995/6 *Family Resources Survey*

Table 4.4 Tenure type by lifecycle groups

| | | | | | Lifecycle group | | | | | |
	Young singles	Older singles	Young childless couples	Lone parents	Young couples, young children	Older couples, young children	Couples, school-age children	Older childless couples	Pensioner couples	Single pensioners	All
Tenure:											
Owner/mortgage	60	59	75	31	68	85	81	83	75	53	66
Rent	39	40	23	69	30	13	18	16	24	45	33
Other	1	1	1	0	2	2	1	1	1	2	1

Source: 1995/6 *Family Resources Survey*

Table 4.5 Housing wealth grouped around the non-zero median by lifecycle groups

Column percentages	Young singles	Older singles	Young childless couples	Lone parents	Lifecycle group Young couples, young children	Older couples, young children	Couples, school-age children	Older childless couples	Pensioner couples	Single pensioners	All
% with housing wealth:											
Le 0	89	54	36	75	39	24	25	21	27	54	48
>0 but <52294	10	25	60	16	48	39	33	31	23	19	26
£52,294+	1	21	4	10	14	37	42	48	51	26	26

Source: 1995/6 *Family Resources Survey*

Table 4.6 Housing wealth grouped around the non-zero median by age groups

Column percentages	16–19	20–29	30–39	40–49	Age groups 50–59	60–69	70–79	80+	All
Housing wealth:									
Le 0	100	78	45	33	30	34	43	51	48
>0 but <52294	0	21	41	31	27	23	21	17	26
£52,294+	0	1	15	36	44	43	36	32	32

Source: 1995/6 *Family Resources Survey*

reached in the repayment of their mortgage. Pensioner couples, older childless couples, older couples with pre-school age children and couples with school age children all had substantial amounts of housing wealth. The age analysis shows that housing wealth increased with age, reaching a peak at the age of 50–59 (see Table 4.6). This peak can be attributed to a number of possible explanations. Families aged over 59 are less likely to have bought homes in the past when public housing and private rented accommodation were more readily available. Alternatively, older groups may be shifting down the housing market and selling up for cheaper homes. This may be because older families need less space once children have left home, or because they need the extra finances to boost their own low incomes or to help out their children.

Figure 4.2 shows median housing wealth by lifecycle group. Four groups – single pensioners, lone parents, older single people and young single people – have zero median housing wealth (that is, at least half of the people in these groups have no housing wealth). This demonstrates, again, that housing wealth is strongly associated with being part of a couple. Pensioner couples have highest median housing wealth – at £59,000, followed by older childless couples (£48,000) and couples with school-age children (£44,000).

Accumulating housing wealth

In the qualitative research, most people had accumulated housing wealth by taking out a mortgage. When doing so, few shopped around. Some of the older people remembered how they had felt little consumer power in relation to the bank or building society manager:

> It is such a different world [today] ... but I [got a mortgage about 40 years ago] when the banks were marble fronted and the bank manager, who nobody knew, you never saw him. He was a god figure in the background that everybody was petrified of ... the building societies were the same, you were thankful that you got a mortgage and that were it ... they were doing you a tremendous favour!

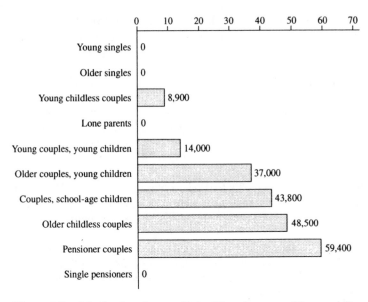

Figure 4.2 Median housing wealth by lifecycle groups (thousand £)

Some of those who had taken out mortgages more recently were more able and willing to flex some consumer muscle. Most, however, either went into the building society of which they were already customers or approached a company recommended by parents or friends.

Endowment or repayment

Those interviewed who had taken out a mortgage before the 1980s had generally taken out repayment mortgages, but some of these people were encouraged in the 1980s to transfer to endowments. One respondent explained how they had begun with a repayment mortgage in the early 1970s (interestingly, they called it a '*straight mortgage*') but had then transferred to an endowment. They subsequently felt that they had not been told of the disadvantages of endowments and now regretted having made the switch. Another couple also regretted moving from a repayment to an endowment mortgage.

Those who had taken out mortgages in the 1980s and early 1990s had generally taken out endowments but the tide clearly turned against endowments during the early 1990s. One couple had begun with an endowment but transferred to a repayment mortgage after having doubts about their initial choice:

> *We had one where we had – like an insurance policy and you were only paying the interest, nothing coming out of the capital. But we panicked a bit, you know and we changed it back over which I was glad we did because now they're saying that there might not be enough in the pot at the end to pay off your mortgage – that, I think, would worry a lot of people.*

Another couple in their 20s had taken out a mortgage in 1996 and had decided to have a repayment mortgage with a fixed interest rate because they thought that this would be more secure:

> *We didn't want any risk and we wanted to know exactly how much it was going to be for quite a long time because it's a big step for us. We didn't want it to go up and we couldn't afford it so we fixed it for 5 years.*

There was a general view that, in recommending endowments, companies had been more concerned with their own interests – and commission – than in their customers' interests. This contributed to general scepticism about financial companies. Respondents felt particularly upset about the inability to trust companies with regard to mortgages since home-ownership was such an important aspect of their lives and they themselves had little real understanding of mortgage schemes.

PENSION WEALTH

Like housing, pensions are also an increasingly important type of wealth. Life expectancy is increasing – the life expectancy of a man aged 65 in 1991 was 15.5 years and for women it was 21.5 years (Hancock *et al,* 1995) – and so there is now a greater length of time when people will be drawing a pension. According to the General Household Survey (GHS), 60 per cent of men in full-time employment had an occupational pension in 1994 and 28 per cent had a personal pension. For full-time working women, the figures were slightly lower, at 53 per cent and 20 per cent respectively, and for female part-time employees the figures were 19 per cent and 11 per cent (Office of Population Censuses and Surveys, 1996). As mentioned before, we use the term 'private' pension to mean both occupational and personal pensions.

Membership of occupational pension schemes is closely linked to income and socio-economic group. According to the GHS, more than three-quarters of full-time working men who earned more than £300 a week (gross), had an occupational pension, compared with only 19 per cent of those earning between £100–£150. About three-quarters of professionals, employers/managers and intermediate non-manual workers had an occupational pension, compared with only about half of male manual workers.

There is less of a difference if we look at personal pensions. These pensions may be much less beneficial to members because there is seldom any employer contribution, so it seems that those in lower-paid jobs, self-employment and in lower socio-economic groups have less paid into their pensions and so do not get the same benefit as those with occupational pensions.

These figures tell us who *has* a private pension but not how much money they have in the pension, so it is very difficult to measure pension wealth. The Inland Revenue (1994) estimates that in 1991 there was £605 billion in occupational pension wealth and £698 billion in state pension wealth.

Pension wealth is therefore substantial, but many people believe that they are not putting enough money into a pension. According to a survey carried out by Hancock *et al* (1995), about two-fifths of those who considered their likely future pension entitlement to be inadequate said that they would not or could not save anything extra towards their retirement. Most of these people were unwilling, rather than unable, to pay more but those who most needed to pay more were least able to do so. Those under 35 were more likely than average to say that they would pay more into their pension, but this then begs the question as to why they were not already doing so, and it should be remembered that a stated willingness or intention does not necessarily mean that the person will carry out any particular act. The authors point out that the working lives of men are getting shorter as they leave school later and retire earlier. This means that time spent contributing to a pension scheme is similarly shortened. Although women's employment and pension contributions have increased, it is estimated that even by 2020 between a half and two-thirds of women will not be entitled to the full-rate state pension (Hancock *et al*, 1995)

A picture of pension wealth

For the purposes of this study, pension wealth is understood to be the wealth based upon contributions made by a person, or made for a person, to date. In other words, it captures what a person should be entitled to, were the pension provision to cease further operations tomorrow but were to honour obligations already entered into. Some studies have calculated pension wealth in other ways, for example by estimating what a person's lifetime pension wealth might amount to, given their present and past situations. Our study is measuring pension wealth to date rather than any future projections. In any calculation of pension wealth a large number of assumptions need to be made and our assumptions are listed in detail in Appendix A. The compexity of these calculations means that any estimate of pension wealth must be treated with some caution.

According to analysis of the 1995/6 FRS, pension wealth, from both state pension and private pension provision, represented the largest source of assets for each lifecycle group – with a median of £22,900 and a mean of £43,600. Mean state pension wealth amounted to £23,900 and mean private pension wealth (including both occupational and personal pension wealth) amounted to £19,700. This means that 55 per cent of all pension wealth is in the state system but state pension wealth is a particularly widespread form of wealth and so if we look at typical portfolios of wealth, the state pension accounts for, on average, 75 per cent of families' pension wealth (see Chapter 2.2 for more discussion of typical portfolios).

Although many families had no housing wealth at all (and some even had negative housing assets), and although many had no financial assets, almost all had at least a minimal accumulation of pension assets. To have no pension wealth at all, not even assets from a state pension, individuals would have had to be outside the labour force or they would not have undertaken any paid work which brought them above the Low Earnings Limit (LEL) and

Table 4.7   Pension wealth by lifecycle groups

	Young singles	Older singles	Young childless couples	Lone parents	Young couples, young children	Older couples, young children	Couples, school-age children	Older childless couples	Pensioner couples	Single pensioners	All
						Lifecycle group					
All pension wealth											
Median wealth	1,000	27,100	4,600	3,300	6,700	17,500	22,200	48,400	95,600	53,200	22,900
Mean wealth	2,500	40,800	7,700	9,400	11,500	25,700	33,400	71,900	121,300	66,500	43,600
Private pension wealth											
Median wealth	0	900	600	0	0	5100	7000	18100	23600	1800	800
Mean wealth	1000	18300	3200	3100	5100	13100	17900	41700	53200	20000	19700
State pension wealth											
Median wealth	1000	18000	3300	3600	4900	10200	12500	25900	70400	46900	14100
Mean wealth	1500	22400	4500	6300	6400	12600	15400	30200	68100	46600	23900
N	5,420	3,837	1,335	2,033	2,327	872	3,309	4,753	3,029	4,570	31485

Source: *1995/6 Family Resources Survey*

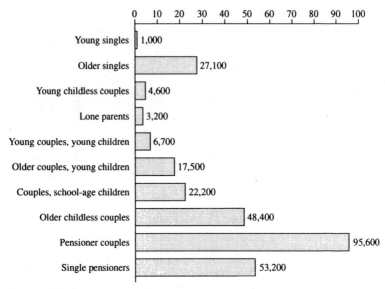

Source: 1995/6 *Family Resources Survey*

Figure 4.3   Median pension wealth by lifecycle groups (including state
and private pension wealth) (thousand £)

they would not have been registered unemployed or on income
support. As a result, families with no pension wealth would be,
for example, divorced women who had not worked in the labour
market or who had worked but whose wages were under the LEL
due to part-time employment perhaps.

Table 4.7 and Figure 4.3 show the amount of money that
different lifecycle groups had in pension wealth. Not surprisingly,
groups with lowest pension wealth were younger people. Young
single people had an average (mean) of about £2,500 in pension
wealth (including state pension wealth). Half of this group had
less than £1,000 in pension wealth. Lone parents and young childless couples also had relatively small amounts of state or private
pension wealth (with median pension wealth of about £3,000 and
£5,000 respectively). The group with the most pension wealth was
pensioner couples (a median of about £96,000) followed by single
pensioners (£53,000) and then older childless couples (£48,000).

Some of these figures appear to be very high but, as shown in
Table 4.7, most pension wealth was in the form of state pension

Table 4.8 Typical portfolios of pension wealth by lifecycle groups

	Young singles	Older singles	Young childless couples	Lone parents	Young couples, young children	Older couples, young children	Couples, school-age children	Older childless couples	Pensioner couples	Single pensioners	All	Mean Value
						Lifecycle group						
Column percentages												
% of pension wealth which is typically .. (£)												
State	87	72	71	90	71	63	62	60	68	81	73	23,171
Personal	1	1	2	0	3	3	2	2	2	0	1	706
Occupational	10	25	21	8	21	29	31	36	30	18	23	18,778
AVC	0	1	1	0	1	1	1	1	0	0	1	213
SERPS	2	2	6	2	5	5	4	2	0	0	2	722
N	5,420	3,837	1,335	2,033	2,327	872	3,309	4,753	3,029	4,570	31,485	

Source: 1995/6 *Family Resources Survey*

assets. Table 4.8 also shows that, as we saw in Chapter 2, state pension wealth was, on average, more important for younger and older groups; who had very low and high pension wealth respectively. Families with the lowest levels of pension wealth had higher proportions of that wealth coming from the state scheme. For example, on average, 90 per cent of the pension wealth of lone parents and 87 per cent of that of single people under the age of 35 came from the state. The modest remainder of their pension assets came, in the main, from occupational pensions. Their lack of occupational pension wealth is a further indication of their exclusion from employment and their dependence on the state. So whilst having no job has the short-term effect of lower income levels and lower standards of living, having no paid work also has severe longer term repercussions. If people remain out of jobs or in lower paid jobs with no occupational pension, younger people and lone parents face a bleak future.

State pensions also typically accounted for the vast majority of pension assets of single people aged over 64 (81 per cent). This figure was substantially higher than that for retired couples. Part of this difference may be due to the differing gender groups and ages of these two lifecycle categories. Single pensioners in the sample were more likely to be women than men and were somewhat older than the pensioner couples. A third of the single people were aged 80 or more, compared with only 14 per cent of the pensioner couples. Over a third of the couples were under 70 years of age compared with only one fifth of the single people. It would be expected that the state pension would play a more important role in the pension wealth of older people. Occupational pensions and personal pensions increased their importance more recently. Before this, the state pension would have been the only way most people accumulated pension assets. Alongside this clear cohort effect, there is also a gender effect at work – these older single people were, in the main, female. Older women have had fewer years of employment than their male counterparts and have had more interrupted employment careers. Further, fewer women's jobs have occupational pensions and women in part-time jobs are even less likely to have an occupational pension available to them (Davies and Ward, 1992; Ginn and Arber, 1996; Martin and Roberts, 1984). Many of the women in the single pensioner category were, no doubt, widows, and so would be living on widows' pensions too.

The pattern seen thus far, whereby state pension formed the bulk of pension assets whilst occupational pensions formed most of the remainder, was apparent across all lifecycle groups. Four groups emerged in which occupational pensions accounted, on average, for a substantial one third of total pension assets. These were, in order of the contribution of the occupational pension, older childless couples aged 35 to 64, couples with school-age children, pensioner couples and older couples with pre-school age children. As we saw in the section on income, these lifecycle groups will have had a longer and a stronger attachment to the labour market. Thus, it is expected that they would have had more access to employers' pension schemes. As a result, those with higher earnings and greater financial security over their working lives are destined to have higher incomes and greater financial security into their old age.

The other aspects of pension wealth, namely personal pensions, assets from additional voluntary contributions to a pension scheme and SERPS pensions, contributed much less to overall pension resources, once again because of cohort effects. Personal pensions were most important, just, for young couples with pre-school age children and older couples with pre-school age children. But, at only 3 per cent of total wealth, personal pensions formed only a small amount of current assets. It is expected that this contribution will grow in the future if young families continue to take out personal pensions and if the younger families today retain their personal pensions.

SERPS pensions were more common for younger families too. Young childless couples and, again, the young couples with pre-school age children and older couples with pre-school age children had higher levels of SERPS-related pension wealth than other families (about 5 per cent). The impact of AVCs on pension assets was negligible for all families. Very few people had made contributions and the contributions made by those who had contributed were low.

As mentioned at the beginning of this section, estimates of pension wealth are highly complex and must be treated with some caution. If we compare our estimates with data from the Inland Revenue (1994) we find that our estimates appear to under-estimate private pension wealth (though not hugely). However, this would be expected because Inland Revenue figures are based on wills subject to probate and are therefore biased towards those with greater wealth and hence more private pension wealth.

Building up private pension wealth

While the quantitative research considered both state and private pension provision, the qualitative focused exclusively on private pension wealth, because the key issue for the qualitative research was decision-making with regard to pension wealth and few decisions are made about state pensions, which are a form of compulsory saving.

Reasons for poor pension coverage

Most people who were interviewed in-depth felt that the state pension would not be enough to meet their aspirations, but nevertheless they felt that they were not paying, or had not paid, enough into a private pension. Young people said that this was precisely because they were young and they wanted to enjoy life a little before worrying about their retirement. They had every intention of paying more into their pensions later on in their lives. One person said that she was waiting for someone to tell her to pay more into her pension and she would do so:

> At the moment I'm quite happy with what I'm paying in and I don't want to increase the size of my payment but I know that next year or the year after I've got to do something to top it up because it's always going to be left behind ... until someone comes, like the insurance man comes and knocks on the door and says, 'hey, you ought to think about upping it because you're not going to have enough.'

Families with children said that there were too many other demands on their money:

> We were talking to the adviser and he said, realistically, you've got to be talking about at least £150 a month just to say that you're going to have anything to live on, you know. And I thought 'Oh, God! There's no way!' because we're still paying the mortgage and we've got the kids to see to ... if he wants to go to college they're now talking about we might have to pay for that tuition.

The consequences of poor private pension provision can be seen to some extent among the pre and post-retirement groups. Those in the pre-retirement group felt that they had not paid enough into their pensions, either because they had started too late or because they had paid too little from early on, but they also believed that it was too late to do much about it now. A married couple had compounded their problems by deciding to 'cash in' their pensions when they moved jobs. The money had now been spent, much to the regret of the respondents. The post-retirement group told a similar story: they generally said that they had not saved enough money but that they had not been able to afford to pay any more during their working lives.

Other reasons for poor private pension provision were that people lacked confidence in such schemes. Some people said that they would pay into a private pension if they were certain to benefit from it, but with scandals surrounding the Maxwell pension scheme and the selling of personal pensions, there was little faith in such schemes.

Taking out an occupational pension

Most respondents had taken out a private pension when they joined a firm which offered an occupational pension. Some of these said that the scheme had been compulsory and they would not have joined a pension scheme otherwise:

> *I'm in a company pension ... it was obligatory that you joined when you joined the company. If I hadn't been in the company pension I don't know if I ever would have got round to doing one at – I'm 24 now ... Most of my friends who aren't in a company pension haven't – I can't think that any of them have a personal pension themselves and I think I'd be the same, because you think £50 is a lot of money every month – I might not even ever see it!*

As with some aspects of financial saving, there is also an accidental or passive aspect to private pension provision. Employers offer schemes and so employees take advantage of them. The fact that they have advantages over personal pensions in terms of employer contributions was not the main reason why people join occupational rather than personal pensions – it was the fact that it was simple to join (in fact, it was often more difficult not to join). Money was taken out of the salary before wages were paid, and the employee generally trusted the employer to provide a decent scheme. There was some general mistrust of all private pension providers, but the people interviewed generally had more faith in their employer's provision than in going direct to a company or broker to take out a personal pension.

Although respondents knew that their employer was paying something towards their pension, they were rather vague about how much this was. Some respondents were concerned about their lack of information about the benefits from their pension and would have liked more but others took an 'ignorance is bliss' approach and were happy to trust that their scheme was fine.

Taking out a personal pension

A smaller group of people were paying into personal pensions. One of these also had an occupational pension but had been concerned that the scheme was not a very secure one and so took out an additional savings scheme to supplement it. Another respondent with a personal pension had no access to an occupational pension and took out his personal pension after he started a family.

There were particular concerns about personal pensions, which respondents felt lacked the security of occupational schemes. Some people felt that they may have been 'ripped off' by advisers and did not understand the scheme enough. They thought that this made it difficult to plan for their retirement because they did not know how much money they could expect to receive from their personal pension. Job insecurity and low wages also meant that there was little money to invest in a pension.

Private pensions and gender

Private pensions were much more common among men in couples than among women, especially with pensioner couples. This was mostly because these women had no access to occupational pensions – they were either at home with their children for most of their adult lives or, where they were or had been in paid work, their employer did not provide them. Where they were currently provided by their employers, women often said that they could not afford to contribute. But it is interesting that in the case of a married couple where a man supplemented his occupational pension with a personal pension, the woman had no private pension provision in her own name even though she did have access to an occupational pension and it would probably have been better financially, if she had made use of it.

It is also interesting that a woman whose partner had taken out a personal pension (because he had no access to an occupational pension), talked about 'our pension' rather than his pension. Whereas occupational pensions were seen more individually, a pension which was paid for out of joint income and perhaps even decided on jointly, was seen more as a joint asset even if it was in one person's name. Most women without pensions were keen to have one if they had access to a 'decent' scheme and if they 'could afford' to pay into it.

Most of those in the pre- and post-retirement groups knew whether their husband's pension was transferable to them in the event of his death and, in some cases, widows were receiving income from their deceased partner's pension. In some ways, these women, especially those from middle class backgrounds, were relatively well off and felt quite independent now that they had their own income.

There were some signs of generational changes in the study, with younger women having better coverage and thinking quite seriously about pension arrangements. One young woman had been particularly determined to arrange a 'decent' pension, having seen her own mother's insufficient income on retirement:

This happened with my mum – she didn't have a pension where she worked and she had to take out her own private one. And I think now she hasn't got enough pension or something, or it's very little. And she said 'I'm so pleased you got into a firm who's got a pension plan'.

5

Conclusions

The findings presented in this book give new estimates of the distribution of wealth using data which is more up-to-date and robust than any previously used. The book also contains important new insights from the qualitative research. But to some extent, things haven't changed: there are still great inequalities in wealth between different income and lifecycle groups. For example, in 1995/6, those with a gross annual income of less than £5,000 had median total wealth of about £3,000. Those on incomes of over £35,000 a year had median wealth of about £110,000. This inequality was partly related to age and lifecycle factors: younger people had lower incomes and lower assets compared to older people; but some groups, such as pensioner couples and single pensioners, were quite likely to be 'wealth rich but income poor'. And other groups, such as young single people and young childless couples were quite likely to be 'wealth poor but income rich'. The richest families, in terms of both income and wealth were older childless couples, and the poorest families were young single people and lone parents.

These conclusions discuss a number of issues: the relationship between income, wealth and the lifecycle; attitudes to wealth; the importance of housing and pension wealth; incentives and disincentives to accumulate wealth; the factors which affect asset accumulation; and ways of enabling people to build up assets. The analysis is based on the 1995/6 *Family Resources Survey* and in-depth interviews among 40 families. The sample size of the qualitative research means that the attitudinal findings cannot be assumed to be representative of the attitudes of people generally.

However, the findings are indicative of attitudes among the general public.

A lifecycle perspective

As we saw in the introductory chapter, there is now great diversity in lifecycle patterns. Some people still leave education, get a job, get married, have children and then see their children fly the nest before they retire. But the growth of cohabitation, childlessness, divorce and lone parenthood mean that lifecycle trajectories are much less certain than they were in the recent past. Nevertheless, the lifecycle is still an important factor in relation to wealth.

Young single people under the age of 35 were, on average, a very poor group in terms of both income and wealth. This is to be expected given that, according to lifecycle theory, young people will have had little time to accumulate wealth and should see their earnings increase as they get older. It is of concern, however, that a fifth of the income of this group typically came from state benefits – if young single people are unable to get a foot on the labour market ladder at an early stage, they may not be in a position later on to gain from higher wages. Although this group were generally poor, analysis showed that a minority were on reasonably high incomes; and compared with other lifecycle groups, the 'young single' lifecycle group were very heterogenous (or even polarised) in terms of their income.

Young childless couples under the age of 35 were rather better off than their single counterparts in terms of both (equivalised) income and wealth. This is partly explained by the fact that a much higher proportion of their income was derived from earnings and they were much more likely to have started accumulating housing and pension wealth as well as financial savings. The trend towards having children later in life, if at all, will mean that larger numbers of people enjoy the financially fruitful time when two members of a couple have relatively high incomes from jobs and low outgoings.

Other research has documented the financial costs of having children (for example, Middleton *et al*, 1997). Our study highlights three key factors related to this. First, it is important to know whether the family contains only one adult or two – as lone parent families stand out as among the very poorest groups in terms of both income and wealth. Second, among couples with children, the age of the children makes a difference – generally the existence of pre-school age children means that there is more likely to be only one full-time earner in the couple and this reduces income and therefore ability to accumulate wealth. Finally, the age of a woman in a couple is also an important factor. In couples where women have delayed child-bearing in order to establish themselves in the labour market, the arrival of children appears to have less of an impact on income and wealth.

The qualitative research emphasised the difficulties that families with children faced in accumulating wealth, given the pressures on them to spend money. And the perceived need to provide financial help to children who go to university extends the period in which children are a major source of expenditure. For owner-occupiers, paying the mortgage was a top priority. Pensions were seen as important but not so immediately necessary as other types of expenditure. This highlights the fact that if people do not pay sufficient amounts into a pension before the onset of their childrearing days, they may never accumulate enough to satisfy the kind of living standards that they would like to enjoy in retirement. The problem is that young people do not wish to think about becoming pensioners and want to enjoy their youth. This is all very well but older people also want to enjoy their retirement and cannot turn back the clock with the power of hindsight.

A group which does not fit the classic lifecycle model is older single people aged between 35–64. This will include people who have never married/cohabited and/or had children, as well as those who have separated from partners and now live without any dependent children. The people in this group are in the prime of their working lives and yet their median income was the lowest of any of the working-age lifecycle groups, with two-fifths of their income coming from state benefits. Their levels of housing wealth and financial savings were very low but they had some assets in pension-provision (although most of this derived from the state pension). Whereas young people, lone parents and couples with children are often the focus of research and policy discussion, this group of older single people is rarely discussed and yet they comprise 12 per cent of families. Given their low levels of income and wealth, the prospects for this group in retirement do not look promising.

The final two lifecycle groups are pensioner couples and single pensioners. Single pensioners are more likely to be women than men and are generally older than those in couples. We might therefore expect them to be much poorer than those in couples but, surprisingly, the (equivalised) median income of single pensioners was not much lower than that for pensioner couples. And single pensioners had about half the level of (non-equivalised) assets as the pensioner couples. The mean income for couples is significantly higher however, so there are some very wealthy pensioner couples. Overall, pensioners have the lowest incomes of any group apart from lone parents but they also have the highest levels of wealth.

Knowledge and attitudes towards wealth

According to the qualitative research, people have different levels of understanding about different forms of saving and investment. Those with most knowledge were more likely to be middle class, be actively saving and work in an environment related to personal finances. Those with less knowledge felt less need of information and felt that they had enough for their current circumstances.

There was a general lack of trust in financial advisers stemming partly from personal experience and partly from feelings stirred by controversies surrounding the selling of endowment mortgages in the 1980s and personal pensions in the 1990s.

In terms of their attitudes to savings, mortgages and pensions, some people were *dedicated savers*, who tried to save at all stages of the lifecycle. Many of these people were quite young and recently married and were at a stage in their lives when their income level enabled them to save or embark on a mortgage. Many were driven to careful money management because of deep-rooted feelings of financial insecurity.

Other people were *circumstantial savers* who believed that saving was more important at some points in their lives than others. These people conformed to the lifecycle model of asset accumulation as they lived through 'spend–save' cycles, saving when they could and then spending the money on necessary items such as holidays and things for their children. These people generally had less money than the dedicated savers and so were less able to save at all times.

Very few people said that they 'lived for the day' and never considered saving to be important. A couple of people, however, were *non-savers*. This was mostly because they had no money to save – their situation determined their attitude, rather than vice versa.

Turning now to running down wealth, most people were keen to use up their financial savings during their retirement and were not planning to leave substantial amounts as bequests. But those who owned homes hoped to pass these on to their children. However, they were also anxious not to use up all their savings before they died and so some bequests were likely to occur on top of money left in the form of housing wealth.

Attitudes were therefore partly determined by lifecycle stage but not entirely. Other factors such as class, age, generation and personal experience were also important.

Incentives and disincentives to save

The tax system may provide incentives or disincentives to save generally, or to save in particular ways. But it was clear from the qualitative research that few people understood how the tax system treats different types of assets. There was some vague awareness about the role of National Savings, TESSAs and PEPs, but most people had very little money to save and they preferred to put what little they had into what they saw as more accessible bank and building society accounts.

Some social security benefits are not available to people with certain levels of assets and this may deter some people from saving. But while there was a general awareness of social security rules about savings, those with most ability to save were least likely to need means-tested benefits and so these rules provided little disincentive to save. There was also some awareness about the asset rules around long-term care but there was also no evidence that such awareness had much effect on behaviour. This was mainly because people thought that they were highly unlikely to go into care. Respondents were nevertheless quick to condemn the social security and long-term care rules as penalising thrift.

The importance of housing and pension wealth

Housing and pension wealth are the two most important forms of personal wealth for most people – only 17 per cent of total wealth is in the form of financial savings (if state pension wealth is included in the total). A third of all wealth is in the form of housing wealth and 48 per cent of all wealth lies in pension assets.

Mean housing wealth was £31,700, which rose to £56,900 for pensioner couples. Half of all lone parents and young single people had no housing wealth at all. People were generally very positive about home ownership, but there were many concerns about taking on a mortgage given fears about job insecurity and interest rates. There were particular concerns about endowment mortgages, which many people regretted taking out.

Pension wealth was also closely linked to income, age and the lifecycle. Mean pension wealth amounted to £43,600. Just over half (55 per cent) of this was in the form of state pension assets. Lone parents had a median of only about £3,000 in pension wealth – and, on average, only 10 per cent of this came from private (that is, occupational or personal) pension provision. Most of those interviewed in the qualitative study thought that they were not currently putting enough money into a private pension. This was related to both income and lifecycle factors. For example, young people could have afforded to put more money into private pensions but they wanted to spend and enjoy their money and thought that there was plenty of time before they retired. People with children felt that they could not afford to pay more money into private pensions because of the financial demands of having a family. Those whose children had grown up had more spare cash but felt that it was too late to make a substantial contribution to their future pension.

The compulsory or semi-compulsory nature of occupational pension schemes was valued by many who said that they would probably be saving nothing or very little if they were not 'forced' to do so. Personal pensions were viewed sceptically as there was very little faith in pension advisers. Pensions were generally seen as a man's responsibility but there were some signs of generational changes, with young single women taking pension provision as seriously as young single men.

Factors affecting wealth accumulation

The lifecycle was clearly an important factor in explaining wealth accumulation as young people had less wealth than older ones. There were also some generational differences between the groups. For example, according to the qualitative research, young people generally had much greater awareness of financial products than older groups, and pension provision in the older groups, especially for women, was poor. But the differences *between* lifecycle groups were not, perhaps, as striking as the differences *within* groups. For example, it was confirmed by the quantitative analysis that there was great inequality among young single people. In the qualitative research, this group was clearly divided between some 'high-flying' two-earner couples, in social class AB, who had considerable amounts of financial saving and were already paying large amounts towards pensions and mortgages (mostly in the hope of retiring before the age of 50!) and the much poorer, working class people who had few financial savings and had not begun paying towards a private pension or a mortgage.

The qualitative research found that wealth-accumulation was related much more to situational, structural factors and trigger events than by attitudes. If anything, attitudes appeared to be a reaction to circumstances rather than having an effect on circumstances. Of course, there may be some interaction between attitudes and circumstances, but the major direction of causation appeared to be from general economic circumstances to wealth-accumulation and attitudes. Those with low incomes and little opportunity to build up assets sometimes took more of a 'live for the day' attitude because they had no other choice. Those on very high incomes and with high wealth could afford to choose to be more carefree with their money. In the middle, some people placed more importance on wealth-accumulation than others and it was within this middle group that attitudes made a difference to behaviour with regard to savings, mortgages and pensions.

Building on this, we can summarise the main factors which affect personal wealth accumulation. The main thrust behind wealth accumulation is *ability* to accumulate wealth. This depends on income level, which in turn depends on employment, likelihood of receiving an inheritance, social class and lifecycle stage.

Those with most money left over after paying for basic needs are most likely to accumulate wealth. Inherited money will become increasingly important with the growth of housing wealth.

While ability is the main factor in wealth accumulation, *attitudes* towards wealth play some role. In part, these are determined by ability to save – those with greater ability to save are generally more positive about saving. But there is also some independent effect – those with the same amount of disposable income will have different attitudes to wealth and so accumulate slightly different amounts of wealth, and in different ways, depending on the priorities they place on saving and investing for the future as opposed to spending for current consumption. Attitudes and priorities depend on a range of personal factors such as parental attitudes (which may be either accepted or rejected), personal experience, a quest for security and lifecycle stage (especially marital status).

Along with ability to accumulate wealth and attitudes to saving, *knowledge* about the different ways of accumulating wealth also affects behaviour. But this, again, is partly dependent on ability to accumulate wealth – those with greater ability are more likely to find out about different ways of saving. Knowledge is higher among those who are part of a social network where personal finance is an important issue. Those who work in the financial sector – at all levels – may also have higher levels of knowledge which will affect their behaviour to some extent, regardless of their ability to accumulate wealth. So ability to accumulate wealth affects both attitudes and knowledge but these two also have some independent effect on wealth-building.

The final factor is the *accessibility* of suitable schemes. Some people with little disposable income may have easy access to a suitable way of building up wealth which therefore encourages them to do so. This is particularly true of occupational pension schemes and 'Save as You Earn' schemes. Employment status is more important here than level of income, although level of income, alongside attitudes to saving, will determine the amount of money saved.

To sum up, the lifecycle is a key factor in explaining personal wealth accumulation, but other factors, such as income level, social class, opportunities for inheritance, age, generation and personal experience also play an important role.

Ways of enabling people to accumulate wealth

Sherraden (1991) argues that the wealthy have been given many incentives to save, through tax subsidies on pensions and home ownership, whereas the poorest groups have received little encouragement or help to save. He suggests that this is because governments pursue an income-based policy for the poor but an asset-based policy for the wealthy. He proposes that welfare policy for the poor should be re-focused on asset-accumulation. In the US, Sherraden points to the development of state-sponsored savings plans for higher education as an example of the kind of programme which would help people to save. He argues that these plans should provide special incentives or assistance to encourage poor people to participate in them. His main proposal, however, is the introduction of Individual Development Accounts which would:

- complement rather than replace income-based policy
- be universally available
- (be subsidised more) have higher subsidies for poor people
- involve voluntary participation
- involve shared responsibility – even the poorest would have to match government subsidies for deposits
- be restricted for certain uses such as further/higher education/training, home ownership, capital for self-employment, with heavy penalties for non-designated use
- involve gradual accumulation
- involve a limited number of investment options
- be used to increase economic information and training.

In November 1997, the government in Britain gave more details about its proposed Individual Savings Accounts. These will replace TESSAs and PEPs from April 1999 in an attempt to encourage more people, particularly those on low incomes, to save long-term. The proposals said that there would be an annual limit of £5,000 and a lifetime limit of £50,000. Income would be tax free. Money in the accounts could be accessed immediately without any penalty. When these plans were circulated, however, there was much criticism on behalf of better-off savers who recognised that they would be losing out from the replacement of TESSAs and PEPs with ISAs. Geoffrey Robinson, the Paymaster-General, said:

> The well-heeled have already done very well out of tax shelters. We now have to find a way of distributing tax incentives more fairly and more widely. (Quoted in the *Guardian*, Wednesday 3 December 1997).

The government argued that the key features of the new schemes would be simplicity, flexibility, accessibility and fairness. The details of Individual Savings Accounts were finalised in July 1998 and contain the features set out above. While many of these features (such as instant access) will appeal to low-income savers, the maximum annual subscription of £5,000 will particularly appeal to middle and high-income savers. Thus the accounts have not been targeted specifically at low-income savers and many of those on high incomes will benefit from tax-free interest.

And, of course, incentives to save which are based on tax relief are irrelevant to those on incomes below the tax threshold. Other schemes such as Christmas clubs or credit unions could be developed further to meet the needs of the poorest groups in our society. In December 1998, the government published its long-awaited plans for pension reform (Department of Social Security, 1998). The Green Paper, 'Partnership in Pensions' announced the following key reforms:

- a new state second pension to replace SERPS for savers on less than £9,000 per year
- a new stakeholder pension to provide high quality, low cost and secure second pensions
- rewards for carers and disabled people.

The reforms are not revolutionary and will not compel people to put a certain proportion of any income into pensions. They merely alter and extend the type of second pension which those on low and moderate incomes have access to. The government hopes that by increasing the attractiveness of second pensions, more people will put more money into them. This research, however, suggests that such hopes may be dashed. People may put some more money into these schemes but it is doubtful that this extra money will be enough to provide the kind of living standards in retirement which people want. In the medium- and long-term, the issue of compulsion is likely to return to the policy agenda.

The government's Social Exclusion Unit has also highlighted issues relating to low-income savers in its 1998 report on *Bringing Britain together: a national strategy for neighbourhood renewal*. This report recognised the importance of providing financial services to people on low incomes – for example, by encouraging or strengthening credit unions. So government policy is concerned with these issues but has, so far, only taken a few small steps towards dealing with problems in practice.

According to the research presented in this book the main way to increase personal wealth accumulation is to increase *ability* to save by increasing incomes. There is great income inequality in Britain, which means that many people have barely enough to maintain a decent standard of living in the present, let alone put money aside from their current income towards the future. It is not within the remit of this study to suggest ways of increasing people's incomes, but it needs to be mentioned because of the strong links between income and wealth.

Another way of increasing personal wealth accumulation is to increase information and *knowledge* about different ways of saving and investing. However, most people seemed to have enough information to meet their needs and there is a danger that merely increasing the amount of information available will lead, in perhaps a counter-productive way, to information overload. But some people on low incomes did perceive a need for free, independent advice which was geared to their particular needs. One respondent had a clear view of what was needed:

> *The government should set up a body, a national body, that people can go to who want financial advice and they should advertise it on the television ... it [should be] totally independent and totally free.*

Generally, people have positive *attitudes* towards saving and investing and, given greater incomes, they would accumulate more wealth. However, there is some evidence that people do not always prioritise saving and investment at times in their lifecycle when they have spare cash. For example, young people are generally very positive about saving but they are also keen to spend and enjoy their youth. Retirement seems a long way off and so pension provision is a low priority. Those who had compulsory (or semi-compulsory) occupational pensions were often pleased in retrospect that they had been 'forced' to save towards the future. The issue of compulsion should therefore be considered carefully. National Insurance is already one form of compulsory saving for the future – this could be increased (although the political will and public approval to do this may not exist). Alternatively, any new stakeholder pensions may need an element of compulsion – for example, in terms of minimum contributions levels.

Finally, wealth accumulation is affected by the easy *availability* of suitable savings and investment schemes. Occupational pensions, Share Save schemes and Save as You Earn schemes were popular, partly because of their (semi-)compulsory nature but also because payment into the schemes was taken from the pay packet and so did not appear to detract from possible alternative expenditure. Savers did not have to make any practical effort towards the, sometimes painful, process of putting away current income towards future consumption.

The importance of wealth

This book ends where it began – by emphasising the importance of wealth in any study of welfare and inequality. Compared with income, relatively little is known about the distribution of wealth and the effect it has on people's lives. Government policies with regard to pensions and Individual Savings Accounts are now placing asset accumulation firmly on the agenda. And the New Labour philosophy of 'stakeholding' also recognises the importance of building up wealth. If the Labour government are to win their 'struggle against poverty and inequality' (from Prime Minister Blair's speech to the Labour Party conference in 1997, quoted in *The Times*) then the issues around wealth accumulation and distribution need to be understood further. In particular, the relative liquidity of different forms of wealth may be especially important for those concerned with poverty and an individual's or family's command over resources. Money in the bank may have a very different meaning and 'value' to someone in poverty compared with money tied up in a pension or in property.

Appendix A

Measuring Pension Wealth

This note states the main assumptions made for calculating pension wealth for various types of individual. Pension wealth is understood to be the wealth based upon contributions made by a person, or made for a person, to date. In other words, it captures what a person should be entitled to, were the pension provision to cease further operations tomorrow but were to honour obligations already entered into (i.e. not to renege on an "implicit" or formal contract).

Individuals can accrue pension wealth from a number of sources. Pension wealth can consist of wealth with respect to:

- the basic state pension
- a SERPS pension
- a company/occupational pension
- a private/personal pension.

In addition, total pension assets to date will include any additional voluntary contributions individuals have made to a pension and any pension wealth from arrangements to which they have contributed in the past, but do not currently. The aim in calculating pension assets is to estimate, for those still contributing, the current value of the pension sum accrued to date, and for those drawing a pension, the value of the assets needed to ensure such a pension could be paid for the rest of their life. Note that a person might be contributing to one pension and drawing another pension.

The key formulae utilised in the calculations are the growth equation (i), the discount equation (ii), the formulae for calculating the value at retirement age of pension rights accrued to date under a salary-related scheme (and the basic state pension) (iii), and the formula for calculating the value to date of accumulated contributions under a money purchase scheme (iv).

$$V = \frac{W * F * S}{-r} * e^{(-r(D-65))} - \frac{W * F * S}{-r} \qquad \text{Equation (i)}$$

$$Total(n) = T(n-1) + [W(n-1)^* X](1-r) \qquad \text{Equation (ii)}$$

$$A = \frac{V}{e^{(rt)}} \qquad \text{Equation (iii)}$$

$$V = Ae^{(rt)} \qquad \text{Equation (iv)}$$

V is the future value of pension assets, A is the current value of pension assets and t is the number of years until an individual reaches retirement age.

W is gross wage, where $W(t=n)=W(t=n-1)*(1+w)$ and w is the rate of increase of wages for the year in question.

S is years of service and D is age of death (taken as 80 for men and 85 for women).

r is a real interest rate which differs for each equation — in equations (i) (iii) and (iv), r is 7%, in equation (ii) r is 5%.

F is the accumulation factor — ie, the proportion of the salary paid in a pension for each year of service under a salary-related scheme (1/60 or 1/80).

T is total amount saved under a money purchase scheme and the interest earned upon it.

X is the contribution rate (employer and member combined) for a money purchase scheme.

The basis for the imposed assumptions is as follows:

Age of death, from mortality tables suggesting life expectancy of people reaching age 65.

r at 7%, in line with long-term rates of growth on a mixed equities/bond portfolio.

r at 5%, convention.

Accumulation factors, based upon information from NAPF and GAD surveys.

CURRENT PENSION SCHEME MEMBERS

This section deals with the assets in the scheme of which the individual is currently a member and with entitlements acquired in schemes in which people have been in the past, but are no longer members.

1) Employer pensions based on individuals' final salary

To calculate pension wealth from a Final Wage scheme, it is necessary to calculate:

- how many 1/60 individuals have received to date
- how many years remain until retirement age, assuming retirement age will be 65

a) Contracted out final wage pension schemes

If pensions are based on final wage and they are contracted out of SERPS, F is assumed to be 1/60 and equation (iii) is used to calculate pension wealth at age 65. This is then discounted back using equation (ii).

b) Contracted in final salary pensions

If individuals' pensions are based on final wage and they are contracted in to SERPS, pension wealth is calculated as above, but F is assumed to be 1/80. Subsequently, pension assets from SERPS (see 2c) will be included.

2) Money Purchase Pension/Personal Pension/SERPS

Where pensions are based on Money Purchase Plans, or are Personal Pensions or SERPS pensions, it is necessary to:

- calculate how much pension individuals have contributed to date
- calculate how much this contribution would buy individuals when they reach the age of 65
- then, discounting back to today's values, calculate what this future pension wealth is actually worth today.

In each case, a certain percentage (X) of the salary is taken to have been contributed. The basis on which contribution rates were calculated is described in Appendix A1, below.

a) Contracted out money purchase pensions and personal pensions

A percentage (X) of salary is contributed to a pension for each year the individual is in the pension scheme. This contribution is paid by the employer and/or the employee. Hence, it is first necessary to know the value of individuals' salaries for all years that they have been in the scheme. This information is not available in the FRS. However, current salary is known. It is possible, therefore, to estimate salaries in previous years by assuming that salary grew according to average earnings increases each year. Current salary was deflated back to estimate a person's salary in 1994, 1993, 1992 and so forth, for each year of scheme membership.

The next step was to calculate total accumulated pension contributions by summing the pension contributions of each year. Equation (iv) gives total assets after n years of service, and this is discounted back using equation (ii).

b) Non-contracted out money purchase pensions

Where the pension is contracted into SERPs (as are many occupational money purchase schemes) a SERPs pension is added (see later).

c) Past occupational pensions

The assets accrued from membership of previous schemes were calculated for those respondents who had been members of past schemes but who were neither currently drawing on those previous pensions nor had cashed in the previous pensions.

i) Past pensions from current employer schemes

Unfortunately, no pension information was available on a small number of individuals who were not currently in their employer's scheme but had belonged to it in the past, had kept the right to this scheme and were not drawing the pension yet. This group has a deferred pension from their current employer of unknown size. However, this group amounted to only 3% of all current employees. (Their maximum age was 66, 58% were women, 83% were in a couple and they were predominantly middle aged or younger).

ii) Past pensions from schemes with previous employers

To calculate this pension wealth, relevant individuals were divided into seven groups, as follows.

Group 1 were employees who were in a current employer's scheme but, in addition, had been in a scheme of a previous employer. Furthermore, they had retained the rights to the previous scheme but were not drawing on this pension yet. This group, in effect, contributed to a previous scheme in which pension assets built up each year until the year that they left that previous scheme. Group 2 employees were similar to Group 1, but did *not* retain their rights to the previous employer's scheme and instead transferred their assets into their current employer's scheme. Group 3 employees were those who had transferred the rights from their previous employers scheme into a PP. Group 4 were employees who are not in their current employers scheme, but they were in a scheme with a previous employer, had kept rights to the previous scheme and were not yet drawing a pension. Group 5 employees were similar to Group 4, but differ in that they did not keep the rights to their previous scheme and, instead, transferred the rights to a PP. Group 6 were currently self-employed but belonged to a previous employer's scheme, kept the rights to the scheme and were not yet drawing a pension. As a result, Group 6 had deferred rights to a previous employer's scheme. Group 7 were self-employed people who transferred their previous employee scheme rights into a PP.

The method for calculating each group's pension assets is described in more detail in Appendix 2.

d) SERPS Pensions

The procedure for calculating assets from pensions contracted into SERPS is as above but here years of service are, effectively, years in employment. Years in employment are assumed to be years in full-time work (years in part-time work are unlikely to have accrued pension credits). If information on years in full-time work is missing, years since the age of 18 are used instead. However, for SERPS pensions, when T is calculated (and in the V and A equations), the interest rate, r, is 2.5% (assumed to be the long-term rate of growth of the economy, the appropriate growth rate for a PAYG pension). This rate is used for discount purposes, too (to avoid the present value becoming negative), so that equations (i) and (ii) are not needed.

3) Basic State Pension

The state pension supposes 44 years of NI contributions after the age of 16. However, some missing years of contributions are allowed such as years in education. Problems in calculating state pension assets only really arise for those with broken labour market careers. This group will consist, in the main, of women with children.

To calculate the basic state pension it is necessary to know

- the number of years of contributions.
- whether the person has acquired any Home Responsibilities Protection (HRP). HRP helps certain groups of people to satisfy their NI contributions when they are outside employment by reducing the total number of years for which they have to make contributions. The major group entitled to HRP are women looking after a young child.

In effect, women are entitled to one year of HRP for each year that they have a child aged sixteen or under. However, only the years from 1978 count and the maximum allowable HRP for women is nineteen years (for men it is twenty-four years). the level of pension for which the person is eligible (pensions for people with dependants are higher than those for single people).

Equation (iii) is used to calculate the value of assets required at 65 to purchase an income at the relevant pension level, and this sum of assets is discounted back using equation (ii).

National Insurance Contributions (NICs)

i) Single men and women with no children
A full labour market history or NI contribution record from the age of 16 is assumed. In n years in the labour market, individuals will have accumulated n/44 of their state pension, which is worth £Z (see below) a week. This pension is payable at the age of 65.

ii) Women with children
The maximum possible years of contribution are 44, but this differs for some women. The number of years required are 39 for women born in 1950, 40 for women born in 1951 and so on, up to 44 years for women born in or after 1955. If women pay NICs in their own right, they are entitled to HRP. As a result, women's years in the labour force are assumed to be the sum of their full-time years and any years of potential HRP - taken to be one year if they had a child aged 16 or less after 1978. If women's NICs are greater than zero, and they are currently part-timers (working 16 hours or less per week), then part-time hours are counted in the years of employment too. However, if NI contributions are zero, then part-time years are not counted. Individuals earning below the Lower Earnings Limit pay no NICs. Analysis showed that the NIC cut off point was around the part-time, 16 hours a week, divide in the FRS. Hence it was assumed that part-timers working fewer than 16 hours a week paid no NICs.

The pension rate - Z

Single men receive the single person's pension, Z=£58.85. Married men, if their wife does not contribute NICs, receive a double persons pension, Z=£58.85+35.25. A married man whose wife is contributing receives a single person's pension, Z= £58.85. Single women who do not contribute NICs receive no pension, Z=0.

Many married women will not be paying the full NIC contribution and so will not receive a full pension in their own right. It is assumed that women marry at the age of 25. So, women who married pre-1978 will be aged at least 42 by 1995. Hence, it is assumed that any married women older than 42 in the FRS have paid a reduced rate of NICs and so will not get a pension in their own right. Married women aged under 42, if their NICs are greater than 0, are assumed to receive full state pensions.

PEOPLE RECEIVING PENSIONS

For these people, it is simply necessary to calculate what would buy current pension income until death using equation (iii). However (current pension income) replaces (W*F*S). If individuals are aged 85 or older, D-65 is set as 0 so that, in effect, these people have no pension wealth.

APPENDIX A1: CALCULATING X CONTRIBUTION RATES

X is the percentage of the individual's salary which is contributed to the pension arrangement. It consists of an employer's contribution (e1) and a member's contribution (m1). The maximum possible value for m1 is set at 15%, in accordance with current tax law (values greater than 15% are set at the mean of non-zero contributions).

a) for occupational money purchase schemes

The amount an individual member contributes to a pension each week is available in the FRS. Let this member's contribution as a percentage of current wage be m1. If the pension is non-contributory and contracted out, the employer contribution (e1) is 9.2% of current wage. If the pension is non-contributory but not contracted out, e1 stands at 7.6% of wage (Note: SERPS will be added later). If the pension is non-contributory and it is not known if it is contracted out, let e1=8.7%. If the pension is contributory, let e1=2*m1. Thus, total contribution= e1+m1, noting that m1 can be zero.

Enhancements to the contribution rate through AVCs are dealt with below.

b) for personal pensions

The individual's statutory contribution (m1) is 1.8+0.6% (=2.4%) for earnings greater than the Lower Earnings Limit (LEL) and lower than the Upper Earnings Limit (UEL). For all earnings over the UEL, the individual does not pay any further contributions. The employer's statutory contribution (e1) is 3% of earnings for *all* earnings above the LEL. Total statutory contribution=e1+m1.

If individuals are self-employed and took out their PPs in 1988 or later, X is calculated as above. However, if the start date of the PP was before 1988, the self-employed can have been contributing larger amounts to a PP. Hence, for these individuals, let the value that they contribute to a PP be equal to the amount that they say they contribute to a PP in the FRS.

Any further member contribution is treated as if it were an AVC (see below).

c) for SERPS

If an individual's pension is contracted in to SERPS, SERPS is treated as if it were a Personal Pension scheme. So, X% for SERPS is calculated as for a PP. However, let m1=1.8% excluding the 0.6%. Total contribution=e1+m1, where e1 is as for a PP.

Additional Voluntary Contributions (AVCs)

a] Employer pensions

If individuals have a current employer pension and if they contribute AVCs , their AVCs may be deducted from their salary or, alternatively, AVCs may be paid directly by the individuals.

* The main group with AVCs (Group 1) had contributions deducted directly from their wage and so the size of deductions was available in the FRS. The amount deducted weekly for AVCs stood at approximately 5% of usual earnings. Note: The sum of total AVC contributions (Z) and members' contributions (m1) are forced to be less than or equal to 15% of salary.
* A second group paid AVC contributions themselves. Therefore, there was no information on the size of their contributions in the FRS. It was decided to set their Z equal to the mean Z% of Group 1.

AVCs are then treated as occupational money purchase pensions. However, the assumption is made that individuals only contributed AVCs for half the years that they were in the pension scheme.

b] Personal pensions

Individuals who said that they have, at one time, had a PP are focused upon.

Group 1 The first group of employees paid extra contributions to a PP in the previous 12 months. The mean value of their contributions, Z, was approximately 2.4% of income. It was assumed that they paid these AVCs for half the years that they were in the PP scheme.

Group 2 This group of employees had not paid any extra contributions in the last 12 months but they had paid extra contributions to a PP in the past. Hence, it was assumed that Group 2 paid half the mean AVCs percentage contribution of Group 1 for each year that they were in the PP scheme.

Group 3 They consisted of self-employees who had contributed extra to a PP in the last 12 months. As the $X\%$ contributions of the self-employed are highly skewed, for those who answered that they did contribute AVCs in the last 12 months, their contributions in AVCs were set as one-quarter of the actual amount in pounds that they contributed normally. Note: if the self-employed took their PP out before 1988, then their total PP contribution can be greater than 15% and so is not maximised at 15%.

APPENDIX A2: DEALING WITH ENTITLEMENTS FROM PAST PENSIONS

Group 1: To calculate assets from this earlier scheme, it is necessary to know salaries for the years of membership of the previous schemes. This information is not available in the FRS and was imputed as follows:

a) it was assumed that end salary in a previous job was 10% lower than the starting salary of the current job
b) current salary of present job is known. It was deflated using average wage rates to find wages for previous years in the current job.
c) as there was no information on number of years with current employer, it was assumed that individuals were in their current job for the length of time that they were in their current employer pension scheme.
d) wages earned in the starting year of the current job were estimated and then used to calculate the final salary of the previous job. It was assumed that individuals were in the previous employers scheme for half their maximum possible labour force years before they started their current jobs. This maximum number of years are the years between the age of 18 and the year employees began their current job. It is assumed that one-sixtieth of salary would have been contributed to the previous scheme for each of the years of membership. On leaving this previous scheme, individuals would have, in effect, accumulated enough pension assets to buy a certain level of salary for a number of years in the future. This value of pension assets is assumed to have appreciated at the RPI rate, capped at 5% per year. A final lump sum of wealth can then be calculated.

Group 2: As above, it was assumed that this group were in their previous employer's scheme for half the maximum possible years; that is half the years between the age of 18 and the year employees began their current job. In addition, it was assumed that the scheme they were in was identical to the one they are in now. This assumption means that this group have simply boosted their current scheme assets by this extra number of years.

Group 3: They are also assumed to be have been in the previous employer scheme for half the number of years between the age of 18 and the year they began their current job. It is assumed that they were in the previous scheme in the years before they joined the current scheme. On leaving the previous scheme, they had a lump sum (calculated using Equations i, i) and iv) which they then put into a PP. This lump sum will have grown - at the rate of a PP (7%) each year after they left their previous scheme.

Group 4: As this group are somewhat similar to Group 1, it was assumed that they were in a previous scheme the same length of time as Group 1. Hence, the mean of Group 1's length in the previous scheme was found and set to be the length for Group 4.

Group 5: It was assumed that they were in the scheme for the same length of time as Group 4 (mean of Group 1), but as they transferred the lump sum to a PP, the lump sum was dealt with as a PP (see Group 3).

Group 6: They were dealt with as were Group 1.

Group 7: They were dealt with as were Group 5.

Appendix B

Measuring Housing and Related Assets

This note outlines the main assumptions made for calculating housing wealth and the value of certain insurance and endowment policies.

Housing assets

Housing assets are the market value of a property minus the amount owed against the house, normally in the form of a mortgage.

a) Value of property

Respondents with a mortgage were asked to estimate the value of their share of the house or flat: *If you were to sell your house/flat tomorrow how much do you think (your share in) it would fetch?* There were a number of respondents for whom this information was missing and, further, this question was not asked of those who owned their homes outright. However, the council tax bands of the homes of those with mortgages and owner-occupiers were available (Note: no information was available on second homes).

A regression model with estimated value of the property as dependent was constructed for those with non-zero housing assets and who did not own their homes outright. Simply including council tax bands as independent variables gave an Adjusted R^2 of 0.56 (variables for region were entered but they did not improve the fit of the model). This model was then used to predict the value of property for all those who had a mortgage or were outright home owners.

To be deducted from the value is the amount still owed to a mortgage lender. The procedure adopted depended upon whether the mortgage was an endowment or a repayment mortgage.

b) Value of endowment policies

Most endowment policies are used to pay back mortgages. These pay out a lump sum at the end of a period. In 1983 MIRAS led to an increase in endowments from about 20% to approximately 70% of mortgages. A year later, life assurance was removed from endowments and so the attraction of endowments declined. However, the legacy has lived on - although endowments are less popular now than they were in the 1980s and early 1990s. Most endowments taken out over 7 years ago are likely to over-shoot. Those taken out in the last 5 years are in danger of under-shooting. Many unit-linked policies are currently behind target, so more will have to be paid to cover the capital sum owed.

Endowment policies can be basic or with profit:

1) basic – if the individual dies, for example, only the payments are paid back.
2) with profit – a bonus and the sum is returned (with profit endowments can be low cost or low start).

Most endowment policies are with profit. A basic sum is assured and a basic level of bonus is anticipated. Endowments incorporate an integral falling protection (i.e. less is paid out late in life, should sudden death occur). With profit endowments are of two kinds:

i) A basic sum is insured, profits are added and there is usually a terminal bonus. The final value should be more than enough to cover the capital owed on a mortgage. The surrender value might not represent the full value of the policy, but account would normally be taken of the proximity to termination and so some proportion of the termination bonus would normally be included.
ii) Unit linked – most endowment policies are unit linked today. The premium covers the charges and life cover. The remaining premium buys units in funds which are then invested in a portfolio. Each month the life assurance cost – that is the

protection element – decreases, since the amount to be paid out falls. Since the policy is unit linked, individuals receive at the end of the period the then value of the units. They are not transferable and the surrender value is the current value of the units.

For the purpose of the project, and because further information was unavailable, it is assumed that all endowment mortgages are with profit.

In calculating the surrender value of endowments, a nil allocation period of 5% of the total full life of the endowment was assumed to go towards administration and commission rather than building up the fund. That is, the original term of the mortgage was found and the premiums for the first 5% of the term were ignored. Savings were only allowed to begin after this time. A rate of return (r) of 7.5% was assumed.

Net housing assets of people with endowment mortgages were thus calculated as:

Housing assets – mortgage debts + the current value of the endowment policy

Housing assets were calculated as above, debts are the amount borrowed, and the value of the endowment policy at time t is:

Endowment (t) = Endowment (t-1)+[premium*(1+r)]

Here the premium is the sum paid annually into the endowment policy.

c) Value of repayment mortgages

In repayment mortgages, the mortgage repayment pays off interest and a part of capital. A repayment mortgage has a capital interest curve. This is a curve from 100% borrowed at the start down to 0% at the end.

An 8% interest was assumed. Since annual mortgage repayment premia go towards paying off both interest and capital, it was estimated that 5 percentage points would be used to pay the interest on the loan, leaving 3 percentage points to pay off the capital debt. With repayment mortgages, assets are constant over time but debts decline each year – by 3 percentage points of the premium. Therefore, net mortgage assets are calculated as: *Assets – Debts* where assets are the value of the property and debts are current capital debts.

People with repayment mortgages are also normally required to take out a Mortgage Protection Policy (MPP) which will pay off the mortgage if the borrower dies (in the 1960s, the role of the MPP was taken by life insurance policies).

Mortgage Protection Policies

For those who had an MPP covering redundancy or sickness/accident, the value of the MPP was calculated as the sum required to buy nine months of mortgage payments. MPPs covering 'death only' were treated differently. On death, an MPP pays out the full sum of mortgage debt remaining and so these very high amounts would skew housing wealth if calculated at face value. They have a current value only if they can be resold, although opportunities for this are very limited. Accordingly, death-only policies have been ignored.

It was found that those who said in answer to the survey that their MPP was death-only had higher repayments than those with other, more all-encompassing MPPs. Further, some MPP payments were very high. MPP payments for more than death normally range from 3% to 5% of outgoing mortgage payments and an average mortgage of £50,000 today has MPP payments of up to £25 per month. But, for example, there was a maximum reported MPP of approximately £300 a month (this was probably because the value of payment was 'amount of last payment').Therefore the MPP payments in the data were capped at the minimum of this normal MPP range and values in excess of 5% were checked to see if they were likely to be 'one-off' payments. It was assumed that anybody with an MPP premium below the lower limit had only a life assurance policy.

Other insurance

Information is available in the FRS on the amount of 'other' deductions from wages. 'Other' includes deductions such as premia to insurance policies. These could be:

Industrial insurance. This is actually a form of 'Life insurance' and it amounts to one of the only ways certain groups of people actually save (ie those with lowest incomes, older people). However, industrial insurance is decreasing in popularity due to the costs of door to door selling and as the population is moving over to bank accounts. On average, contributions to industrial insurance policies amount to approximately £10 for a 4-weekly month.

Life assurance. This has two forms: protection in case of death and as a method of saving. Before 1984, life assurance premium relief was available (tax relief on those of about 15%). Since 1984, with the abolition of premium relief, it became questionable how efficient this savings scheme was. Now, life assurance is mostly used to pay off a mortgage or as a 'baby bond'. Before the expansion of PEPs, life assurance was used instead of AVCs or pension plans as a way of soaking up 'spare money' or saving. The most common life assurance policies are *Flexible Whole of Life Policies,* whereby the policy holder can vary what proportion is going into the savings and protections aspects of the policy. At the beginning of the policy, individuals may stress the protection aspects whilst they have young children, for example, stressing the savings aspects when children have left home.

However, while the FRS provides information on the total amount for 'other' payments, we do not know how much was for insurance policies, and if so what kind of policies were being referred to, how long they had been operating and so on. For these reasons, the assets associated with such insurance policies could not be measured.

Appendix C

Qualitative Fieldwork Details

The main objective of the qualitative research was to understand how and why people make decisions about building up and running down assets. Within this there were a number of specific aims:

- To explore knowledge about different savings, mortgages and pension schemes.
- To find out from where people get advice from about assets and whether they feel they have enough information.
- To investigate attitudes towards building-up and running down different types of assets.
- To chart actual experiences of building-up and running down assets.
- To determine levels of awareness of incentives and disincentives to build up and run down assets.

The study involved in-depth interviews with 40 households across a range of lifecycle groups in four areas of the country. These areas were chosen to reflect different types of locality – an inner city area in a major northern conurbation, a suburb of a Midlands city, a rural area in the Midlands and an affluent city in the South.

THE SAMPLE

Recruiters were employed to obtain the sample of people to be interviewed for the study. The sample for this project consists of people in four 'lifecyle' groups. These were:

Group 1: Young people, no children

single people or couples; aged 20–35; with no children; at least one person in full-time employment in the household.

Group 2: Families with children

couples or lone parents; aged 35–45; with dependent children in the household – ie aged under 16 or in full-time Further Education, *not* Higher Education; at least one person in full-time employment in the household.

Group 3: Empty-nest families

couples or single people; aged 45–64; with no dependent children *living* at home; at least one person in full-time employment in the household.

Group 4: Retired people

couples or single people; aged 65 or over; at least one retired person in the household.

We interviewed 10 respondents in each of these four lifecyle groups. There were also quotas on social class such that of these 10 respondents:

- roughly half were from social classes A,B or C1
- roughly half will be from social classes – C2, ,D
- *at least* half will be owner-occupiers

Social class was based on occupational details. Thus ABs are professionals and senior managers, C1s are other non-manual workers, C2s are skilled manual workers and Ds are semi-skilled manual workers. Retired people are classified according to the main occupation of their working life.

Fieldwork took place in four areas: an inner city of a major Northern conurbation; a suburb of a Midlands city; a rural area in the Midlands; and an affluent Southern city. A mix of different respondent types were recruited in each area.

RECRUITMENT, CONTACTING AND INTERVIEWING

The recruiters we employed worked for MORI. Their performance was co-ordinated and supervised by MORI's Area Managers and any problems were picked up and dealt with by them. Most interviewees were recruited on the doorstep but some were recruited in the street.

Recruitment began during the first week of July in 1997. The recruiters were fully briefed before they went out into the field. They were using a recruitment questionnaire (see Appendix D) which ensured that the people interview fitted in with the quota.

All potential respondents who fitted the recruitment criteria were presented with a letter on PSI headed notepaper, giving them some information about PSI and the study, asking them to participate in the research and reassuring them of confidentiality. If they were willing to be interviewed the recruiter arranged an appointment and left the respondent will be left with a written note of the time and date of the interview. All appointments were confirmed by the recruiter the day before the interview was due to take place.

All four interviewers working on the project were briefed in July 1997 and the fieldwork period began directly after the briefing. Interviewing took place at the end of July and throughout August. All interviews were tape-recorded and transcribed. Respondents were given £10 as a thank-you for their time.

Fieldwork Documents

RECRUITMENT QUESTIONNAIRE

Hello, I'm _____ I work for MORI and we're carrying out a survey about peoples' knowledge about different ways of saving money. Can I ask you a few questions?

1.   People have very different attitudes towards saving for the future. Can you tell me which of the following statements comes closest to your attitude to saving?

You should live one day at a time and worry about the future when you get there.

It's always important to think about the future and save for a rainy day.

2.   May I just check who shares this household with you? Do you live with _____

Husband/wife/partner	1
parent/parent in law	2
children aged under 16	3
children aged up to 20 but still in full-time education	4
other people	5

3.   How old are you (and you partner)? [Show card]

	Respondent	Partner
Up to 19	1	1
20–35	2	2
36–45	3	3
46–64	4	4
65+	5	5

4.   Are you (and your partner) currently working? [Show card]

	Respondent	Partner
Working full-time (30+ hours)	1	1
Working part-time	2	2
Not working – retired	3	3
Not working – other	4	4

5.   Social class – basic MORI questions on: type of job; level of education and/or training required; size of organisation; whether or not supervising others

6.   Do you own this house or are you renting it?

Own outright	1
Have mortgage	2
Rent – council/Housing Association	3
Rent – private landlord	4
Other	5

Check whether eligible for interview, if appropriate...

The Policy Studies Institute would like to ask you more about your views and experiences of different methods of saving. [Encourage respondent to take part]. I've got a letter here which tells you a bit more about the study and a leaflet about the Policy Studies Institute. When will it be convenient for an interviewer to call?

Topic guide

A   KNOWLEDGE ABOUT SAVINGS, MORTGAGES AND PENSIONS

QA1   What are the different ways in which people can save or invest money or build up assets?

[Probe fully open-ended]: What others?
[Then prompt for each of these using showcard 1]:

Q   Which of these have you heard of?
     Financial savings   –   bank, building society savings accounts
                        –   national savings, premium bonds
                        –   other accounts such as TESSAs PEPs
                        –   stocks, shares, bonds, unit trusts
                        –   insurance or endowment policies
     Taking out a mortgage to buy your own house/flat
     Taking out a personal or occupational pension

Q   How much do you feel you know about each of these? [Prompt for each]

QA2   How do people find out about saving schemes, mortgages and pensions?

[Probe open-ended]: What other ways?
[Then prompt]:

     –   from professionals – bank/building society/financial adviser/ employer eg re: pension
     –   reading newspapers/magazines
     –   informally – friends, family

Q   What are the advantages and disadvantages of each source of information?

Q   Where do you get most of your information from?

Q   Do you feel you have enough information about what is available? what particular kind of extra information would you like?

B   ATTITUDES TOWARDS SAVINGS, MORTGAGES AND PENSIONS

QB1   To begin with, can you tell me which of the following options comes closest to your attitude to saving?
      [Showcard 2]
      You should always try to save money for a rainy day
      You should save money at some stages in your life but not all the time
      You should live for the day and not worry about saving for the future
      [Prompt] why do you say that?

Q   Have you ever felt differently in the past? When? Why change?
      [Prompt as appropriate]
      – attitude when young and single
      – attitude when married
      – attitude when had children
      – attitude when children left home
      – attitude when retired

Q   Why do you think you have this point of view?
      [Prompt] Influence of parents, age, family status, employment status, other experience

[If has partner]
Q   How does your partner feel about saving?
      do you have separate savings? Why?

Q   Do you think you might feel differently in the future?
      [Prompt] what stages (see list above), why?

QB2   How financially secure do you feel at the moment?
      – why is that?
      – how do you feel about that?

       – how secure is your/partner's job at the moment?
       – how do you feel about that?
       – how important is it to you to feel financially secure?
       – why is that?
       – does this affect your behaviour about savings, mortgages and pensions

QB3   To what extent have you thought about saving for when you get older?
       – how much money would you like to live on in retirement?
       – do you know what level the state pension is currently paid at?
       – do you think you (will) have saved enough? Why/not?
       – how much would you be willing to pay per month towards a pension?
       – do you think you will need to pay for residential care in your old age?
       – how do you feel about that? Will you be able to afford it?
       – do you know whether a basic level of residential care in old age is available free to everyone or are some people expected to pay towards it? [Probe for knowledge]
       – do you know any of the details?
       – how did you become aware of them?
       – do they affect the way you think about saving?

QB4   Do you anticipate coming into money in the future? Eg Inheriting money, life assurance, insurance policy? How does that affect your attitude to saving/investment?
    [Probe for details] Eg amount, when it might happen, how feel about it etc

QB5   How important is it to you that...
       – you can get at your savings whenever you need to? [Prompt]: Why is that? etc
       – that your money is earning good rates of interest?
       – that the method you've chosen isn't too risky?
       – which of these is most important?

Q If you had the choice of these two investment plans, which would you choose? Both involve investing £100 for a year. [Showcard 3]

  PLAN A - guaranteed to have £110 in a year

  PLAN B - 80% chance of having £110–130 but 20% chance of having £90–£110

  Why?

QB6 What are the advantages and disadvantages of …?

  [Probe fully – especially fopr housing and pensions]

  – having financial savings

  – buying your own home

  – taking out an occupational or personal pension

Q Which (of these) is the best way to save or invest money, in your opinion?

  – Why do you think that?

QB7 The tax system offers some benefits to particular types of saving/investment. Are you aware of any of these benefits?

  – which ones?

  – how did you become aware of them?

  – how do they work?

  – does that make them more attractive to you?

QB8 The social security system has rules about the amount of money you can have in savings or investments if you need to claim social security. Are you aware of these rules?

  – which ones?

  – what are they?

  – how did you find out about them?

  – how does that affect your attitude to saving?

Q Have you ever claimed any benefits, such as Unemployment Benefit, Income Support, Housing Benefit, Retirement Pension? Do you think you might in the future? Do you think you would have too much money saved to be entitled?

C EXPERIENCES OF SAVINGS, MORTGAGES AND PENSIONS

Financial savings

QC1   What forms of financial savings do you and your partner have at the moment?

[Prompt using showcard 1] for financial savings. [If yes]:
- how long have you been saving that way? [Year and lifecycle stage]
- why did you choose that method at that time?
- did you get any advice when you began saving? Who from? How helpful?
- do you feel you know enough about the scheme? Eg interest rate?
- roughly how much do you save/how often?
- how long do you think you'll keep saving that way?
- what are you saving for?
- approximately how much do you have saved and invested?

[Fill in form]

[Prompt in bands of £5,000 if necessary]

[If have partner]: is it in joint names? Why/not?

Mortgages

QC2   Do you currently have a mortgage at the moment? [If yes]:
- how long have you had the mortgage? [Year and lifecycle stage]
- why did you take out a mortgage at that time?
- did you get any advice when you took out the mortgage? Who from? How helpful?
- roughly how much do you pay monthly?
- is it endowment or repayment or other?
- what exactly does this mean?
- do you feel you know enough about the scheme?
- how much is your house/flat currently worth? [Fill in form]
- how much of that have you paid off?

[If have partner]: Is it in joint names? Why/not?

Personal and occupational pensions

QC3 Do you have a personal or occupational pension at the moment? [If yes]:
 – when did you start (paying into) it? [Year and lifecycle stage]
 – why did you start a pension then?
 – did you get any advice when you started paying it? Who from? How helpful?
 – roughly how much do you pay monthly? [Fill in form]
 – how much does your employer contribute towards it?
 – what benefits will you get at the end of the day?
 – what does this depend on?
 – do you feel you know enough about the scheme?

QC4 Are there any forms of saving or investment that you used in the past but don't use now?
 For each method:
 – what type or saving scheme, mortgage, pension is it? [Probe fully for details as above]
 – why did you choose that method?
 – when did you take it out and how long for?
 – did you receive any advice when you took it out? Who from? How helpful?
 – roughly how much did you save/time period
 – when did you stop saving that way? Why?
 – did you receive any advice when you ended it?
 For financial savings:
 – what were you saving for?

[Check if own home outright. If yes, ask]:
QC5 How much is your home worth, approximately? [Fill in form]

[Check if receiving personal or occupational pension. If yes, ask]:
QC6 How much has you pension been worth? Lump sum? Weekly payments? [Fill in form]

ALL
QC7 What other financial assets do you have? How much are they worth approx? [Fill in form]

QC8 Has the amount you have saved or invested been affected by changes in the level of your income? In what way?

Q   At what stages in your life has income changed and affected savings/investment?
     – how much has it increased or decreased?

QC9 Are there any forms of saving/investment which you don't use now but think you might use in the future? [Showcard 1]

For each method   – why don't you use it now?
                         – why might you use it in future?
                         – when do you think you might start?
                         – would you seek advice about it? Who from?
For financial savings: – what might you save for?

[All don't have/never had/ won't have savings/mortgage/pension
QC10 Why don't you have savings/mortgage/occupational pension?

D RUNNING DOWN SAVINGS AND ASSETS

QD1 What would you do if you needed to get hold of some money in a hurry?
     – borrow, use savings, something else
     – why?
     – how would this vary depending on the amount of money needed?

QD2 How likely is it that you'll want to spend all or some of the money you've saved or invested some time in the future?
     [Prompt]:
     – when? how much?
     – in what circumstances?
     – why? What for?
     – why not before?

QD3 How would you go about getting hold of your money?
- would it be easy/difficult?
- would you lose out financially?
- how would you feel about that spending your savings?

QD4 Some people free up some of the money they've invested in their housing by 'trading down' and buying a less expensive property or selling and moving into rented accommodation. Are you planning to do this/have you done this?
- when would you consider it?
- why/why not?
- how would you feel about it?
- how would you go about doing it if you wanted to?

Q Would you consider/have you ever considered taking out a second mortgage to release some of your assets? Why/why not?

Q There are some schemes, called Home Care Plans or Equity Release Schemes, which help people to stay in their own homes while releasing some of the equity in their home. Have you heard of such schemes? What do you think of the idea?

QD5 Some people cash in pensions or insurance plans before they've matured because they need to get their hands on money quickly. Are you planning to do this/have you done this?
- when would you consider it?
- why/why not?
- how would you feel about it?

QD6 Are you planning to use up all your assets during your lifetime or are you planning to leave some money to other people, such as children and other relatives?
- How much are you planning to leave? Why? Who to?

E CONCLUSION

QE1 What sort of things would encourage more people to save

and invest more money?
  – better information
  – tax incentives
  – removal of social security/long-term care disincentives
  – would that encourage you to save more

QE2 What sort of information do people need to make decisions about savings and investment?
  – who should provide it?
  – what form should it take?
  – key points that people need to know?

QE3 Anything else you like to say about savings and investments?

SHOWCARD 1

Financial savings
    Bank and building society savings accounts
    National savings
    Premium bonds
    TESSAs
    PEPs
    Stocks, shares, bonds, unit trusts
    Insurance/endowment policies
    Other financial savings
Paying towards a mortgage to buy your own home
Taking out a personal or occupational pension

SHOWCARD 2

You should always try to save money for a rainy day
You should save money at some stages in your life but not all the time
You should live for the day and not worry about saving for the future

SHOWCARD 3

Invest £100 for one year

PLAN A
Guaranteed to have £110

PLAN B
80% chance of having £110–130
but 20% chance of having £90–110

References

Atkinson, A (1971) 'The distribution of wealth and the individual life-cycle' *Oxford Economic Papers 23*, Oxford: Oxford University Press

Atkinson, A, Gordon, J and Harrison, J (1986) *Trends in the Distribution of Wealth in Britain 1923–1981*, STICERD Discussion Paper, London: LSE

Atkinson, A and Harrison, G (1978) *The Distribution of Personal Wealth in Britain*, Cambridge: Cambridge University Press

Banks, J (1997) 'Tax incentives for saving: the UK experience' Institute for Fiscal Studies home page, http://www1.ifs.org.uk/research/PensionsAndSaving/taxIncentivesForSaving.HTM

Banks, J and Blundell, R (1993) *Household saving behaviour in the UK*, Institute for Fiscal Studies Working Paper no W93/5, London: IFS

Banks, J, Dilnot, A and Low, H (1994) *The distribution of wealth in the UK*, London: IFS

Banks, J, Dilnot, A and Tanner, S (1997) *Taxing household saving: what role for the new individual savings account?*, Commentary 66, London: Institute for Fiscal Studies

Barclays Life (1996) *Pensions research: closing the misery gap*, London: Barclays Life

Beck, U (1992) *Risk Society: towards a new modernity*, London: Sage Publications

Bernheim, B (1987) 'Dissaving after retirement: testing the pure lifecycle hypothesis' in Bodie, Z, Shoven, J and Wise, D *Issues in Pension Economics*, Chicago: University of Chicago Press

Bernheim, B and Scholz, J (1992) *Private saving and public policy*, National Bureau of Economic Research, Working Paper no 4215

Berthoud, R and Kempson, E (1992) *Credit and Debt*, London: PSI

Boadway, R and Wildasin, D (1994) 'Taxation and Savings: A Survey' *Fiscal Studies*, vol 15, no 3, pp19–63, London: IFS

Bull, J, and Poole, L (1989) *Not rich, not poor – a study of housing options for elderly people on middle incomes*, SHAC/Anchor Housing Trust

Burgoyne, C and Morison, V (1997) 'Money in remarriage: keeping things simple' *The Sociological Review*, vol 45 no 3, pp363–95

Cagan, P (1965) *The effect of pension plans on aggregate saving*, New York: Columbia University Press

Davies, B, and Ward, S (1992) *Women and Personal Pensions*, Equal Opportunities Commission, London: HMSO

Department of Social Security (1996) *Family Resources Survey*, Great Britain 1994–95, London: HMSO

Department of Social Security (1998) A new contract for welfare: Partnership in Pensions, Cm 4179

Dex, S (1987) *Women's Occupational Mobility*, London: Macmillan Press Ltd

Dex, S (1992) 'Labour force participation of women during the 1990s: occupational mobility and part-time employment' in R M Lindley (ed) *Women's Employment: Britain in the Single European Market*, Equal Opportunities Commission, London: HMSO

Disney, R, Gallagher, T and Henley, A (1995) *Housing assets and saving behaviour among the elderly in Great Britain* Institute for Fiscal Studies Working Paper no W95/22, London: IFS

Dunn, A and Hoffman, P (1983) 'Distribution of wealth in the UK: the effect of including pension rights and analysis by age group' *Review of income and wealth*, pp 243–82

Dunn, A and Hoffman, P (1978) 'The distribution of personal wealth' in *Economic Trends*, vol 301, pp 101–18

Duvall, E (1971) *Family development*, Philadelphia: Lippincott

Fagan, C and Rubery, J (1996) 'The salience of the part-time divide in the European Union', *European Sociological Review*, December

Finch, H and Elam, G (1995) *Managing money in later life*, London: HMSO

Feldstein, M (1974) 'Social security, induced retirement and aggregate capital accumulation' *Journal of Political Economy*, vol 82, pp 905–26

Friedman, M (1957) *A theory of the consumption function*, Princeton: Princeton University Press

Gilly, M and Enis, B (1982) 'Recycling the family lifecycle: A proposal for redefinition' in Mitchell, A (ed) *Advances in Consumer Research*, Vol 9, Ann Arbor

Ginn, J, and Arber, S (1996) 'Patterns of employment, gender and pensions: the effect of work history on older women's non-state pensions', *Work, Employment and Society*, 10, 3: 469–90.

Glover, J and Arber, S (1995) 'Polarisation in mothers' employment' *Gender, Work and Organisations*, 24 October, pp 165–79

Goodman, A and Webb, S (1994) 'For Richer, For Poorer: the changing distribution of income in the United Kingdom, 1961–1991' Commentary no 42, London: IFS

Graham, H (1987) 'Women's poverty and caring' in C Glendenning and J Miller (eds) *Women and Poverty in Britain*, Brighton: Wheatsheaf Books Ltd

Hakim, C (1996) *Key Issues in Women's Work: Female Heterogeneity and the Polarisation of Women's Employment*, London: The Athlone Press Ltd

Hamnett, C, Harmer, M and Williams, P (1989) *Housing inheritance: a national survey of its scale and impact*, Amersham: NHBC

Hancock, R, Jarvis, C and Mueller, G (1995) *The Outlook for Incomes in Retirement*, London: Age Concern Institute of Gerontology, King's College

Harbury, C (1962) 'Inheritance and the distribution of personal wealth in Britain' *Economic Journal*, vol 72

Harbury, C and Hitchens, D (1979) *Inheritance and Wealth Inequality in Britain*, London: Allen and Unwin

Hennessy, P (1995) *Social Protection for Dependent Elderly People: Perspectives from a Review of OECD Countries*, OECD Working Papers, Volume III, No 63, Paris: OECD

Holmans, A and Frosztega, M (1996) *Negative Equity – Information from Household Interview Surveys*, DoE Occasional Paper, June 1996

Inland Revenue (1994) *Inland Revenue Statistics*

Jacobs, S (1997) 'Employment changes over child-birth: a retrospective view', *Sociology*, 31, 3: 577–90

Joseph Rowntree Foundation (1995) *Inquiry into Income and Wealth*, volume 2, York: Joseph Rowntree Foundation

Joseph Rowntree Foundation (1996) *Inquiry into Meeting the Costs of Continuing Care*, York: Joseph Rowntree Foundation

Katona, G (1975) *Psychological economics*, New York: Elsevier

Kemp, P (1982) 'Housing landlordism in nineteenth century Britain' *Environment and Planning*, 14, 1437–47

Kempson, E (1994) *Outside the Banking System*, London: HMSO

Kempson, E and Ford, J (1995) *Attitudes, beliefs and confidence: Consumer views of the housing market in the 1990s*, London: Council of Mortgage Lenders

Keynes, J (1936) *The general theory of employment, interest and money*, London: Macmillan

King, A and Dicks-Mireau, L (1982) 'Asset-holding and the lifecycle' *The Economic Journal*, 92 (June) 247–67

Kurihara, K (1955) (ed) *Post-Keynesian economics*, New Jersey: Rutgers University Press

Lea, S, Tarpy, R, and Webley, P (1987) *The individual in the economy*, Cambridge: Cambridge University Press

McGarry, K and Schoeni, R (1995) *Transfer behaviour within the family: results from the asset and health dynamics survey* National Bureau of Economic Research, Working Paper no 5099

Mack, J and Lansley, S (1985) *Poor Britain*, London: Allen & Unwin

McKay, S (1992) *Pensioners' Assets*, London: PSI

Mackintosh, S, Means, R and Leather, P (1990) *Housing in later life: the financial implications of an ageing society*, Bristol: SAUS

McRae, S (1994) 'Labour supply after child-birth: do employers' policies make a difference?', *Sociology*, 28, 1: 99–122

McRae, S (1997) 'Household and labour market change: implications for the growth of inequality in Britain' *British Journal of Sociology*, 48, 3: 384–405

Macran, S, Joshi, J and Dex, S (1996) 'Employment after childbearing: a survival analysis', *Work, Employment and Society*, 10,2: 273–96

Martin, J and Roberts, C (1984) *Women and Employment: A Lifetime Perspective*, London: HMSO

Middleton, S, Ashworth, K and Braithwaite, I (1997) *Small Fortunes: Spending on children, childhood poverty and parental sacrifice* York: Joseph Rowntree Foundation

Modigliani, F and Brumberg, R (1954) 'Utility analysis and the consumption function' in Kurihara, K *Post-Keynesian Economics*

Mullings, B and Hamnett, C (1992) 'Equity release schemes and equity extraction by elderly households in Britain' *Ageing and Society* 413–42

Munnell, A (1976) 'Private pensions and saving: new evidence' *Journal of Political Economy* 84, 1013, 32

Munroe, M (1988) 'Housing wealth and inheritance' *Journal of Social Policy* 17, 4, 417–36

Murphy, P and Staples, W (1979) 'Family and household changes: developments and implications' *Journal of Consumer Research*, vol 6 (June), 12–22

Office of Population Censuses and Surveys (1996) *Living in Britain: Results from the 1994 General Household Survey*, London: HMSO

O'Higgins, M, Bradshaw, J and Walker, R (1988) 'Income distribution over the lifecycle' in Walker, R and Parker, G (eds) *Money Matters: income, wealth and financial welfare*, London: Sage Publications

Oliver, M, Shapiro, T and Press, J (1993) "Them that's got shall get': inheritance and achievement in wealth accumulation' *Research in Politics and Society*, vol 5, 69–95

Ormerod, P and Willmott, M (1989) 'Willpower – home ownership, inheritance, and the next century' *Poverty*, vol 73, London: CPAG

Osborne, K (1996) 'Earnings of part-time workers: data from the 1995 New Earnings Survey', *Labour Market Trends*, May: 227–35

Pollock, G (1997) 'Uncertain futures: young people in and out of employment since 1940', *Work, Employment and Society*, 11,4: 615–38

Poterba J (1994) 'Introduction' in Poterba J (ed) *International comparisons of household saving*, Chicago: University of Chicago

Ratcliffe, R and Maurer, S (1995) 'Saving and investment among the wealthy: the uses of assets by high income families in 1950 and 1983' *Research in Politics and Society*, vol 5, 99–125

Roberts, K (1984) *School Leavers and their Prospects*, Milton Keynes: Open University Press

Rowlingson, K (1995) *Moneylenders and their Customers*, London: Policy Studies Institute

Rowlingson, K, Whyley, C, Newburn, T and Berthoud, R (1997) *Social Security Fraud: the Role of Penalties*, London: The Stationery Office

Rowntree, B (1901) *Poverty: a study of town life*, London: Macmillan

Royal Commission on the Distribution of Income and Wealth (1977) London: HMSO

Rubery, J, Horrell, S and Burchell, B (1994) 'Part-time work and gender inequality in the labour market' in A. MacEwan Scott (ed) *Gender Segregation and Social Change*, Oxford: Oxford University Press

Sherraden, M (1991) *Assets and the Poor: a new American welfare policy*, New York: Armonk

Schaninger, C and Danko, W (1993) 'A conceptual and empirical comparison of alternative household lifecycle models' *Journal of Consumer Research*, vol 19, 580–94

Spanier G, Sauer, W and Larzelere, R (1979) 'An empirical evaluation of the family life cycle', *Journal of Marriage and the Family*, 41, 27–38

Stears, G (1998) 'The Retirement Survey – the main findings' *Benefits*, Volume 22

Townsend, P (1979) *Poverty in the United Kingdom*, Harmondsworth: Penguin

Walker, R, Hardman, G and Hutton, S (1988) 'The occupational pension trap: towards a preliminary empirical specification' *Journal of Social Policy* vol 18, 4

Warneryd, K-E (1998) *The Psychology of Saving*, Cheltenham: Edward Elgar

Wells, W and Gubar, G (1966) 'Life Cycle Concept in Marketing Research' *Journal of Marketing Research*, 3 (November), 355–63

Wiener, J (1994) 'Private sector initiatives in financing long-term care' in OECD (ed) *Caring for frail elderly people*, Paris: OECD

Whyley, C, Kempson, E and Herbert, A (1997) *Money Matters: Approaches to Money Management and Bill-Paying*, London: PSI